FILING THE
FAFSA

The Edvisors® Guide to Completing the
Free Application for Federal Student Aid

2015-2016 Edition

D0775861

ISBN: 978-0-9914646-3-0

For information, write to Edvisors Network Inc., 10000 W. Charleston Boulevard, Suite 200, Las Vegas, NV 89135.

Edvisors and the Edvisors logo are registered trademarks of Edvisors Network Inc. FAFSA is a registered trademark of the U.S. Department of Education. CSS/Financial Aid PROFILE is a registered trademark of the College Board. Other trademarks are the property of their respective owners.

DISCLAIMER: The information contained in this book is provided for general informational and educational purposes and is not, nor intended to be, legal, financial or tax advice. The authors and publisher are not authorized to practice in front of the IRS and are not subject to IRS Circular 230. This information is general in nature and may not apply to the specific circumstances of individual readers. No claims are made about the accuracy, timeliness or usefulness of the content contained in this book. Readers should seek specific guidance directly from a qualified legal, financial or tax professional. Nothing contained in or provided through this book is intended to be or is to be used as a substitute for professional advice.

This book contains information concerning federal student financial aid programs. While the authors and publisher believe this information to be accurate, this information has not been reviewed or approved by the U.S. Department of Education.

About the Authors

Mark Kantrowitz is Senior Vice President and Publisher of Edvisors.com, a comprehensive web site about planning and paying for college. Mark is a nationally recognized expert on student financial aid, scholarships and student loans. He has testified before Congress about student aid policy on several occasions and is frequently interviewed by news outlets. He has been quoted in more than 5,000 newspaper and magazine articles in the last five years. He has written for the *New York Times*, *Wall Street Journal*, *Forbes*, *Washington Post*, *Reuters*, *Huffington Post*, *U.S. News & World Report*, *Newsweek* and *Time Magazine*. Mark is the author of two bestselling books about scholarships and financial aid, including *Secrets to Winning a Scholarship*, and holds seven patents. Mark is a member of the board of directors of the National Scholarship Providers Association and the board of trustees of the Center for Excellence in Education. Mark serves on the editorial board of the *Journal of Student Financial Aid* and the editorial advisory board of *Bottom Line/Personal*.

In 1996, Mark provided the U.S. Department of Education with a prototype implementation of an online Free Application for Federal Student Aid (FAFSA), including edit checks and skip-logic. This lead to the launch of FAFSA on the Web for the 1997-98 academic year. Since then, more than 100 million people have used the web-based version of the FAFSA.

David Levy is Editor of Edvisors.com. David is a 30-year veteran director of financial aid at some of the nation's leading colleges, including Scripps College, the California Institute of Technology and Occidental College. He is respected by students, parents and financial aid professionals nationwide because of his knowledge of financial aid, his extensive outreach and volunteer activities, and his leadership in helping to simplify the student aid application process. David has served in numerous leadership and volunteer positions with the National Association of Student Financial Aid Administrators, Western Association of Student Financial Aid Administrators, California Association of Student Financial Aid Administrators, the California Student Aid Commission and the College Board. He has received more than 35 awards for his service. He serves as a board member on the Community Foundation of the Verdugos, the Hathaway-Sycamores Child and Family Services and the Oak Crest Institute of Science. He also serves on the editorial board of the *Journal of Student Financial Aid*.

David has served as a technical advisor and consultant for the U.S. Department of Education's FSA Coach, online training materials for student financial aid administrators. In addition, for the past 14 years, he has been instrumental in developing FAFSA guides and PowerPoint presentations for the state-wide California Cash for College efforts which help thousands of students and their families apply for federal, state and institutional student aid each year.

Acknowledgements

A book of this scope is the result of advice and input from many sources.

First, we'd like to thank Jeff Baker, Cindy Cameron, Sue O'Flaherty, Misty Parkinson and other U.S. Department of Education staff. They work tirelessly each year to develop and update the Free Application for Federal Student Aid (FAFSA). We commend their efforts to streamline the student aid application process as they balance the often diverse demands of students, families, colleges and policymakers.

The success of the student financial aid application and delivery of student aid funds processes is due in large part to college financial aid administrators and other professional organizations committed to ensuring student access. We gratefully acknowledge the guidance and counsel we received from the following individuals who reviewed and commented on multiple drafts of Filing the FAFSA: Carlos Adrian (Syracuse University), Phil Asbury (University of North Carolina), Bonnie Lee Behm (Villanova University), David Belanger (Smith College), Nancy Coolidge (U.C. Office of the President), Karen Cooper (Stanford University), Ethel Desmarais (Bryn Mawr College), Jacob Gross (University of Louisville), Verna Hazen (Rochester Institute of Technology), Ron Johnson (UCLA), Heather McDonnell (Sarah Lawrence University), Jon McGee (College of Saint Benedict and Saint John's University), Mary Nucciarone (University of Notre Dame), Michael Scott (Texas Christian University), Kate Peterson (Oregon State University), Barry Simmons (Virginia Polytechnic Institute and State University), Oscar Sweeten-Lopez (Michael and Susan Dell Foundation) and Diane Stemper (Ohio State University). Their close scrutiny of the book was invaluable.

We would like to thank Despina Costopoulos and Bryan Dickason from the California Student Aid Commission along with Alma Salazar, Kelly Reynolds, Paola Santana and David Rattray from the Los Angeles Chamber of Commerce's Cash for College effort. Their feedback and thoughtful questions from the state, high school and community-based organization perspective help us to clarify sometimes ambiguous and conflicting information.

The many questions we have received from students, parents, guidance counselors, financial aid administrators and policymakers have helped us identify potential sources of confusion about the FAFSA. We have attempted to provide clear answers to these questions in this book.

We also appreciate the critical guidance offered by Bart Astor (consultant and retired financial aid administrator), Norman Birnbach (Birnbach Communications), Robert Evans (ATTAIN Financial Aid Management and Student Services (FAMSS)), Cheryl Foster-Hunt (USA Funds), Leo Kornfeld (retired U.S. Department of Education official), Kathie Little (retired College Board official and financial aid administrator), Jim Montoya (College Board), Lynn O'Shaughnessy (The College Solution), Paul Phillips (retired financial aid administrator), Dorothy Sexton (College Board), Robert Shireman (California Completes and former U.S. Department of Education official), Cathy Thomas (retired financial aid administrator) and Patti Winkel (KnowsyMoms.com).

Our co-workers at Edvisors deserve our heart-felt thanks for their enthusiastic support: Jacob Boucon, Mikal Calvert, Nancy Ciccone, Lori Crepas, Michael Dubendris, Len Fainer, John Falb, Chris Hodge, Erik Hutchinson, Joe Kakaty, Erin Leonardi, Michael McGowan, Anita Myles, Jared Norman, Tessie Osmena, Jon Romano, Alex Seda, Barbara Sharpe, Todd Shaul, Joe Taylor, Russ Theriault, Todd Transue, Marianne Worley and Paul Wozniak.

Marianne Worley on the Edvisors team deserves special recognition for sharing her creative design talents in formatting and laying out the book. Her vision and imagination have never failed to impress.

Finally, we convey our deepest appreciation, recognition and love to our families, who sacrificed many hours in helping us bring this year's edition to fruition.

Mark Kantrowitz and David Levy
December 2014

Contents

INTRODUCTION

Paying for college is the second largest expense most families incur, second only to the purchase of a home.

A college education provides many benefits. College graduates earn more money and have lower unemployment rates, on average, than high school graduates. The prospects for future job growth are greatest for jobs requiring a college degree. People with college degrees are also healthier, happier, more likely to volunteer and more likely to vote. College is a pathway to success and a better life.[1]

To go to college, most people need some financial help. Everybody, regardless of income, struggles to pay for college. Even wealthy students need some help. Luckily, there are many sources of money to help students pay for college costs and make college more affordable.

Money for College

Last year, there were more than $248 billion in student financial aid funds available to help students and their families pay for college.[2] About two-thirds of the total, $165 billion, came from the federal government (including $96 billion in federal education loans), $10 billion from state governments, $49 billion from colleges and universities, and $24 billion from private sources (including private scholarships, employer tuition assistance and private student loans).

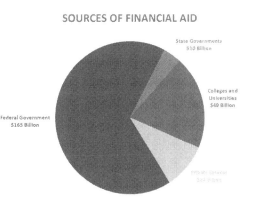

SOURCES OF FINANCIAL AID

State Governments
$10 Billion

Colleges and Universities
$49 Billion

Federal Government
$165 Billion

Private Sources
$24 Billion

There are four major types of student financial aid – grants and scholarships, work-study, education tax benefits and education loans.

Grants and scholarships are gift aid, which typically is money that does not require repayment. Grants are usually awarded based on the student's demonstrated financial need. Scholarships are generally based on merit, such as academic, athletic or artistic talent. More than $100 billion in grants are awarded by the government and colleges each year. Scholarships are available from a variety of sources, including foundations, corporations, private agencies and employers. Scholarships provide about 6 percent of total financial aid awarded to students and about 13 percent of gift aid. To find scholarships, use a free scholarship matching service like StudentScholarshipSearch.com. Another source of scholarship money is ScholarshipPoints.com, where students use points earned completing surveys to enter drawings for scholarships. Beware of services that charge a fee to find or apply for scholarships. If you have to pay money to get money, it's probably a scam.

Work-study programs provide opportunities for students to earn money to help pay for school expenses.

Education tax benefits give families money back on their federal income tax return, based on amounts paid for college costs. These include the American Opportunity Tax Credit, Lifetime Learning Tax Credit, Student Loan Interest Deduction and other tax credits and deductions.

Both students and parents can borrow from a variety of low-interest education loan programs designed to help with the educational expenses of the student. These include loans from the federal government, such as the Federal Stafford loan, Federal Perkins loan and Federal PLUS loan, colleges and private student loans from banks and other financial institutions. Education loans usually do not require repayment of principal to begin until after the student is no longer enrolled in college. Generally, students should maximize gift aid before borrowing money from an education loan program.

Financial Aid Application Forms

The first step in obtaining money to help pay for college is to apply for the money by completing financial aid application forms. These include the Free Application for Federal Student Aid (FAFSA), the CSS/Financial Aid PROFILE, and other forms required by colleges and universities.

The Free Application for Federal Student Aid (FAFSA) is used to apply for student financial aid from the federal government, the state government, and most colleges and universities. It is the main gateway form for obtaining need-based student aid. (Even some merit-based scholarship programs may require applicants to complete the FAFSA, usually to ensure that students receive all the need-based aid to which they are entitled.) The FAFSA is also a prerequisite for obtaining low-cost federal education loans. The FAFSA may be used to apply for financial aid for graduate and professional school in addition to financial aid for undergraduate school.

Every student should complete the FAFSA each year, even if he or she did not get any money last year. The financial formulas are complicated enough that it is difficult to predict whether a student will qualify for financial aid without applying. Even small changes may have a big impact on the amount and types of financial aid the student will receive. Examples include changes in the number of children enrolled in college at the same time, changes in the amount of child assets and changes in the amount of income. Families also have a tendency to underestimate eligibility for need-based aid and overestimate eligibility for merit-based aid.

The FAFSA should be completed by students and their families online, through FAFSA on the Web (FOTW) at www.fafsa.ed.gov. The online form has built-in edit checks to catch common errors, yielding a more accurate determination of eligibility for need-based financial aid. It also has intelligent skip-logic that will omit redundant and irrelevant questions. There's also the IRS Data Retrieval Tool, which applicants can use to transfer information from their federal income tax returns for completing or updating the FAFSA.

The FAFSA should be completed as soon as possible after January 1 of the senior year in high school and each subsequent year in college. (The FAFSA cannot be filed before January 1, as it requires income information from the prior tax year.)

Families should *not* wait until after the student has been admitted by a college or they have filed their federal income tax returns to submit the FAFSA. Several states have very early deadlines for state grants, some as early as February 1. Other states and some colleges award their grants on a first-come, first-served basis, until the money runs out. Don't delay applying for aid. Filing the FAFSA earlier will help students avoid missing deadlines, thereby, maximizing the amount of aid for which they are eligible.

Instead, families should report **estimated** student and parent income information on the FAFSA. Estimates can be based on W-2 and 1099 statements, the last pay stub of the prior year, and current bank and brokerage account statements. (Since 1099 statements must be mailed by mid-February and W-2 forms by the end of January, it is possible that the family will not receive them before state and college financial aid deadlines. In particular, 1099 statements for mutual funds, foreign stocks and real estate investment trusts tend to arrive late.) It's a good idea to review the previous year's federal income tax returns to ensure that no source of income is overlooked. Applicants must correct any inaccuracies later, after their federal income tax returns have been filed, but it is best to have the initial income estimates be as accurate as possible. Otherwise, there will be a significant change in the amount of financial aid eligibility when the FAFSA is updated after the federal income tax returns have been filed.

Example: To receive aid in the 2015-2016 academic year, students will need to complete the 2015-2016 Free Application for Federal Student Aid (FAFSA). The 2015-2016 FAFSA will become available on January 1, 2015. It is important to submit the FAFSA as early as possible after January 1, 2015, but no later than June 30, 2016, to be considered for student financial aid in the 2015-2016 academic year.

It takes about an hour to complete the FAFSA. The FAFSA may be a little time-consuming, but it's not impossible, and can provide thousands of dollars to help pay for college. This guide helps with information and insights about how to complete the FAFSA and maximize the amount of financial aid the student will receive.

The student and at least one of his or her custodial parents whose information is reported on the FAFSA must complete and sign the FAFSA. If the parents have two or more children in college at the same time, each child must complete a separate FAFSA. However, after the FAFSA is filed for the first child, the Confirmation Page allows parents to transfer their financial information into the FAFSA of the student's sibling(s).

The information on the FAFSA is used to calculate the student's expected family contribution (EFC). This is a measure of the family's financial strength and is used to determine eligibility for need-based financial aid, such as the Federal Pell Grant, Federal Work-Study and subsidized federal student loans. Despite the name, the actual cost to the family is likely to be higher than the calculated EFC.

The student will receive a Student Aid Report (SAR) about a week after filing the FAFSA online, two weeks after filing a paper version of the FAFSA. The colleges listed on the FAFSA will receive an Institutional Student Information Report (ISIR) at the same time. The SAR will include the student's EFC and an estimate of the student's eligibility for the Federal Pell Grant and federal student loans.

While most colleges and universities use the FAFSA for awarding institutional aid, some supplement the FAFSA with other financial aid application forms.

- The CSS/Financial Aid PROFILE (http://profileonline. collegeboard.org) form is used by about 250 mostly-private colleges and universities for awarding their own financial aid funds. These colleges and universities still use the FAFSA for federal and state aid. Some scholarship competitions may also require the CSS/Financial Aid PROFILE form.

- Some colleges and universities may require their own financial aid application forms in addition to the FAFSA and PROFILE. These forms may collect information that is not available on the FAFSA or PROFILE, such as questions about unusual family financial circumstances and questions for the non-custodial parent when the student's parents are divorced or separated. These forms help the institution award its own financial aid funds and must be returned to the college or university directly.

There are also many private scholarships, each of which has its own application forms. There is a scholarship application data standard called ScholarSnapp.org that may allow students to reuse information from one scholarship application to another, if both scholarship providers use the standard.

Some colleges will request copies of student and parent federal income tax return transcripts and other documentation to verify the information reported on financial aid application forms. (Using the IRS Data Retrieval Tool at www.fafsa.ed.gov to update the income information on the FAFSA will reduce the likelihood of the student's FAFSA being selected for verification or having to provide a federal income tax return transcript to the school.) It is best for the student and parents to complete their federal income tax forms as soon as possible. Keep copies of these forms along with all tax schedules, attachments and W-2 and 1099 statements, as well as the most recent bank and brokerage account statements.

Also, be sure to submit any required applications and copies of requested documents by the published deadlines. At many institutions, failure to meet a deadline may jeopardize student eligibility for grants and other types of aid. **Don't miss out on college admissions or student financial aid by missing a deadline.**

FAFSA Step-by-Step Guide

This guide provides instructions and tips on completing the FAFSA. The information is presented based on the online version of the FAFSA, also known as FAFSA on the Web (FOTW). The order in which questions are listed in FOTW may differ from the order in the paper version of the FAFSA.

Screenshots are based on the 2015-2016 demo version of FAFSA on the Web.

Please note that any personal information included in this guide does not come from a real student, but instead is part of a composite of several samples provided by the U.S. Department of Education.

Step 1   Getting Ready

Step 2   FAFSA Account Creation and Setup

Step 3   Completing the FAFSA

Section 1 – Student Demographics

Section 2 – School Selection

Section 3 – Dependency Status

Section 4 – Parent Demographics

Section 5 – Student Financial Information

Section 6 – Sign and Submit

Section 7 – Confirmation

Step 4   Next Steps

✦ Edvisors®

FAFSA Application Process

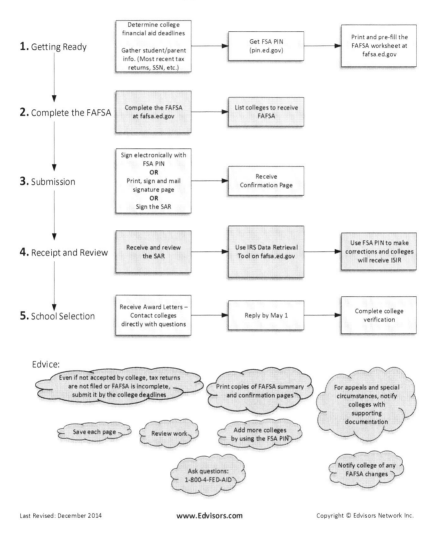

1. Getting Ready

> Determine college financial aid deadlines
>
> Gather student/parent info. (Most recent tax returns, SSN, etc.)

→ Get FSA PIN (pin.ed.gov)

→ Print and pre-fill the FAFSA worksheet at fafsa.ed.gov

2. Complete the FAFSA

> Complete the FAFSA at fafsa.ed.gov

→ List colleges to receive FAFSA

3. Submission

> Sign electronically with FSA PIN
> **OR**
> Print, sign and mail signature page
> **OR**
> Sign the SAR

→ Receive Confirmation Page

4. Receipt and Review

> Receive and review the SAR

→ Use IRS Data Retrieval Tool on fafsa.ed.gov

→ Use FSA PIN to make corrections and colleges will receive ISIR

5. School Selection

> Receive Award Letters – Contact colleges directly with questions

→ Reply by May 1

→ Complete college verification

Edvice:

Even if not accepted by college, tax returns are not filed or FAFSA is incomplete, submit it by the college deadlines

Print copies of FAFSA summary and confirmation pages

For appeals and special circumstances, notify colleges with supporting documentation

Save each page

Review work

Add more colleges by using the FSA PIN

Notify college of any FAFSA changes

Ask questions: 1-800-4-FED-AID

Quick Tips

- When the FAFSA refers to "I," "You," "Your," it is referring to the student (not the parent, family, or FAFSA preparer).

- Always double-check even basic demographic items, such as name, date of birth, Social Security Number, address and zip code.

- Nothing will delay a FAFSA faster than errors or omissions. Check all responses carefully.

- Colors matter and each year's FAFSA is different in color. For the 2015-2016 academic year, student-related items are in yellow and items for the parent(s) to complete are in purple. The Student Aid Report (SAR) matches the color of the student sections of the FAFSA.

- The FAFSA is a free form, as the name suggests. Students do not need to pay to submit or have the form processed.

- Students must reapply for financial aid every year.

- The term "FOTW" refers to "FAFSA on the Web" and is used synonymously with the term "FAFSA."

- File the FAFSA as early as possible!

FAFSA Colors

The color of the parent sections of the FAFSA is always purple.

The color of the student sections of the FAFSA rotates each year among four possible colors:

- Yellow (2015-2016)
- Orange (2016-2017)
- Green (2017-2018)
- Dark Blue (2018-2019)

Browser and Computer Tips

- FAFSA on the Web (FOTW) may be used with the following web browsers:
  - Apple Safari version 4.0 and above
  - Google Chrome version 4.0 and above
  - Microsoft Internet Explorer version 7.0 and above
  - Mozilla Firefox version 4.0 and above
  - Opera version 10.0 and above
  - Opera Mobile

- Macintosh users should turn off virtual memory before using FAFSA on the Web (FOTW). Although the tab key may be used to move from one question to the next, the mouse must be used to select items and to click on buttons on the Macintosh. Also, please select "Yes" for "OK" and "No" for "Cancel."

- Students who are using a public computer to file the FAFSA should close the web browser after they are done. This will erase part of the computer's memory, preventing the next user of the computer from accidentally seeing the student's private information. The web browser may be closed by selecting "Exit" from the "File" menu on Windows PCs or by choosing "Quit" after selecting the browser from the menu bar on Macintosh computers. It is also a good idea to clear the browser's cache of temporary files. An option to clear the cache and other browsing data typically can be found under the Tools or History menu of the browser.

- If accessing the web through a firewall, be sure that the firewall is configured to allow traffic to TCP/IP ports 80 and 443.

- Do not use the browser's back and forward buttons to navigate between pages, as previously posted pages cannot be resubmitted. Use the navigation options built into the form.

Step 1 – GETTING READY

Before starting the FAFSA, students will need to prepare by gathering some personal paperwork, tax forms and other documentation. Students will also need to provide some demographic information about themselves and their family.

All financial information needs to be for the previous tax year, which is usually the previous calendar year. For example, to file the 2015-2016 FAFSA, students will need documentation from the 2014 tax year (January 1, 2014 – December 31, 2014). Fiscal year filers should use the tax year that overlaps the most with the 2014 calendar year.

> TIP: If students and/or their parents (if applicable) have not yet completed their federal income tax returns, or don't have their W-2 tax forms available, they can estimate their income using the last pay stubs of the year. The previous year's federal income tax returns may also be used as a reference if income has not changed by much from last year. The family should use the IRS Data Retrieval Tool to update their financial information at a later date

Families will need these records to complete the FAFSA. Filling out the FAFSA is easier and takes less time if the student and the family gather these records before going online or starting the paper form. Please keep in mind that not all families will have or need all of these records.

The student will need:

- The student's driver's license (if the student has one)

- The student's Alien Registration Card (if the student is not a U.S. citizen but is an eligible non-citizen)

**The student and parents (if the student is a dependent student) will
need:**

- Social Security cards (for the Social Security Numbers) and legal
  names

- W-2 forms, 1099 forms, records of earned income, and records of
  other taxable income such as unemployment benefits

- Federal income tax returns for the prior tax year, if completed (IRS
  Form 1040, 1040A or 1040EZ or the equivalent foreign income tax
  return)

- Records of child support paid, if any

- Records of untaxed income, if any

- Current bank and brokerage account statements

- Records of stocks, bonds, mutual funds and other investments

- Records of student aid funds that were included in adjusted gross
  income (AGI), such as the taxable portion of scholarships and
  fellowships and AmeriCorps benefits

- Records of taxable earnings from Federal Work-Study or other
  need-based work programs

The student and parents will also need a Federal Student Aid PIN to sign
the FAFSA electronically.

**Remember, 2014 federal tax returns do not need to be completed before
applying for student financial aid. It is more important to submit the
FAFSA and other aid applications by the published deadline dates
using estimated data than to wait until 2014 student and parent federal
income tax returns are actually completed. (If the FAFSA is filed with
estimated data, the applicant must correct any inaccuracies after the**

2014 student and parent federal income tax returns have been filed. The federal income tax return data on the FAFSA may be updated using the IRS Data Retrieval Tool at www.fafsa.ed.gov**.)**

For future reference, students should be sure to keep copies of all documents used to complete the FAFSA, a copy of the completed FAFSA as well as a copy of the Confirmation Page and Student Aid Report.

FAFSA on the Web (FOTW)

This guide focuses on how to complete the 2015–2016 FAFSA on the Web (FOTW) – the online version of the FAFSA. There is also a paper version, but almost everybody completes the online form. More than 20 million FAFSAs are submitted online each year, 99 percent of the total number of FAFSAs filed.

The primary benefit of using FAFSA on the Web (FOTW) at www.fafsa.ed.gov is that the processing time is significantly reduced. Students and schools receive a response from the federal processor more quickly. In turn, this helps colleges prepare a more timely notification of eligibility for financial aid. (This is a definite advantage if students are trying to decide between two or more schools.)

Other benefits are:

- Fewer errors on the form. Built-in edit checks will not allow the family to go to the next section if some of the information is incomplete or inconsistent in the current section. Before submitting the FAFSA, the program will do a final review of the entire application, checking for missing and / or conflicting information.

- Thanks to skip-logic, there are fewer questions to complete. This means that students will not be asked questions that do not apply to them. For example, unmarried students will not be asked questions about a spouse.

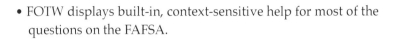

- FOTW displays built-in, context-sensitive help for most of the questions on the FAFSA.

- In many cases, drop-down boxes are provided so the family can choose from a selection of responses.

- Students may list up to ten colleges on FOTW and only four colleges on the paper FAFSA.

Families who have submitted their 2014 federal income tax returns may be able to transfer IRS data directly to the FOTW using a tool called the IRS Data Retrieval (IRS DRT). Using the IRS Data Retrieval Tool may reduce the likelihood that a student's FAFSA will be selected for verification. The IRS Data Retrieval Tool may be accessed through FAFSA on the Web (FOTW) at www.fafsa.ed.gov.

As soon as the FAFSA on the Web is submitted, a Confirmation Page can be printed to instantly verify that the application has been submitted. This page will contain a *Confirmation Stamp* showing the date and time that the FAFSA was successfully submitted.

FAFSA on the Web Worksheet

Besides the FAFSA itself, there is another form that may be useful, but not required – the 2015-2016 FAFSA on the Web (FOTW) Worksheet. The worksheet may be found at www.fafsa.ed.gov (type "Worksheet" into the search box). While the worksheet does not have all the questions students will find on the actual FAFSA, it is a good place for some students and their families

Note: The questions on the FAFSA on the Web Worksheet may not necessarily appear in the same order as on FAFSA on the Web (FOTW) or the print version of the FAFSA. The worksheet also does not contain all of the questions listed on FOTW or the print version of the FAFSA.

to start the process of applying for financial aid. It gives an idea of the type of questions that appear on the FAFSA and the information that will be required. The FOTW worksheet can help families get a head start on completing the FAFSA before January 1.

Federal Student Aid PIN

To take full advantage of FAFSA on the Web, both the student and one of his or her custodial parents must have a Federal Student Aid PIN (personal identification number). The PIN serves as an electronic signature for U.S. Department of Education documents, including the FAFSA. The PIN may also be used to add schools to the FAFSA and make corrections to the FAFSA.

> Do not share the PIN with anybody, not even a relative. The PIN gives access to private information. It can also be used to sign federal education loan documents.

The PIN works like the special number one might have for an ATM card. It identifies the person who is completing the FAFSA uniquely, and functions like a wet signature written with a pen. The student and custodial parent must each have their own PIN. They should each use a different number for their PIN, as, otherwise, the federal processor will flag the FAFSA for identity verification.

Do not share the PIN with anyone. The student should not share his or her PIN with his or her parents, or vice versa. Likewise, do not share the PIN with anyone helping the family complete the FAFSA. Sharing a PIN may invalidate any documents signed with the PIN, including the FAFSA.

If the student or parent have not yet applied for a PIN, the student and one custodial parent whose information is required on the FAFSA should each go to the PIN web site at www.pin.ed.gov. Students and parents can also apply for a PIN when completing the FAFSA on the Web, so they should not worry if they have not yet applied for PINs.

To obtain a PIN, an applicant should provide his or her name, Social Security Number, date of birth and other information on the PIN web site. The name, date of birth and Social Security Number (SSN) must be an exact match to the information on the applicant's Social Security card, or the application for a PIN will be rejected. The U.S. Department of Education will email the PIN within minutes (but only if a valid email address has been provided). The email message will contain a link to a web page that will display the PIN. The link will expire after two weeks (14 days).

The PIN is considered conditional until the PIN applicant's identity has been confirmed with the Social Security Administration (SSA). This can take up to 3 days.

Parents and/or students who do not have Social Security Numbers are not eligible to sign the FAFSAs using a PIN, but can print, sign, and mail a paper Signature Page after completing FAFSA on the Web (FOTW). Directions can be found on the FOTW Signature Page by clicking the "Other options to sign and submit" link.

If a student and parents are unable to print the Signature Page, they can sign and return the SAR after they receive it.

If a student forgets his or her PIN, the student can get the PIN again by clicking on "Request a Duplicate PIN" on www.pin.ed.gov. If the PIN has been compromised, however, the student should select "Change My PIN" to get a new PIN instead. If the PIN has been disabled or locked, the student should select "Reestablish My PIN."

FSA ID

Starting in Spring 2015 (sometime after the April 15 federal income tax deadline), the U.S. Department of Education will implement a new login process for students and parents to access FAFSA on the Web (FOTW). The new FSA ID will replace the Federal Student Aid PIN with a user-selected username and password. This will be more secure, since it eliminates the need for students and parents to provide personally identifiable information (PII), such as their name, date of birth and Social Security Number (SSN), every time they access U.S. Department of Education web sites. This permits self-service password retrieval by email without revealing PII. It also allows for name changes (e.g., through marriage) without requiring an application for a new FSA ID.

The new FSA ID will provides a single sign-on for accessing all of the U.S. Department of Education's consumer-facing web sites. For example, in addition to FAFSA on the Web, the FSA ID can be used to access the National Student Loan Data System (NSLDS), StudentLoans.gov, StudentAid.gov and the TEACH Grant web site. The IRS Data Retrieval Tool will not require students and parents to re-authenticate themselves if they log in with a FSA ID."

The FSA ID username must be at least six alphanumeric characters. The password must be 8-30 alphanumeric characters. The password may not match the individual's name, Social Security Number or date of birth. Everybody will be required to change their password at least once every two years.

Each FSA ID must be associated with a different email address. In particular, the parent and each student must have their own email address. Parents may not use their own email address for a dependent student. The student must have his or her own email address. A new, web-based email account can be obtained for free from Gmail.com, Outlook.com or another free email web site. A test email message will be sent to the email address to confirm its validity.

When choosing a password, remember that the FSA ID is also an electronic signature, used to sign the FAFSA, loan promissory notes and other legal documents. Choose a very secure password. This password should be different than the passwords you use on other web sites or to access your email. Do not use dictionary words, common terms or other easy-to-guess passwords, such as: "password," "abc123," "123456," "12345678," "31415926," "14142135," "27182818," "000000," "111111," "qwerty," "iloveyou," "monkey," "trustno1," "financialaid" or "FAFSA." Do not use your first or last name or a nickname as your password.

Do not use your girlfriend or boyfriend's name. Do not use your date of birth or Social Security Number as your password. Your password should be at least eight alphanumeric characters and preferably more. Include a mix of uppercase and lowercase letters and numbers. Do not substitute numbers for corresponding letters, like 0 for O or o and 1 for l. Do not share your password with anybody.

Overview of the FAFSA on the Web

FAFSA on the Web (FOTW) is a seven-section online form.

Instructions are embedded on each screen of the online form.

Sections shaded yellow on the 2015-2016 FAFSA are for students and those shaded **purple** are for parents.

Important contact information can be found in the instructions.

FAFSA on the Web (FOTW) consists of the following seven sections:

- **Student Demographics** asks for information about the student. **The words "I," "you" and "your" refer to the student applicant.**

- **School Selection** allows the student to have FAFSA data sent to up to ten colleges and universities.

- **Dependency Status** determines whether the student's parents must provide demographic and financial data on the FAFSA.

- **Parent Demographics** collects data about parent household and other parent information if the student is determined to be a dependent student.

- **Financial Information** collects data about student (and parent(s), if applicable) 2014 taxed and untaxed income and assets.

- **Sign and Submit** asks students (and parents, if applicable) if they want the information on the FOTW submitted electronically using their PINs. In addition, it asks those submitting the FOTW about the accuracy of the data. In submitting the FOTW, the student and parent(s) are agreeing that any financial aid funds received will be used for educational purposes only.

- **Confirmation** allows the student to print a Confirmation Page which confirms the submission of the FOTW to the U.S. Department of Education. It also provides other useful information such as the Expected Family Contribution (EFC), estimated Federal Pell Grant and Stafford Loan eligibility, as well as a listing of the schools to which the FOTW information will be sent. For each school listed on the FAFSA, the student will also receive important consumer information including, but not limited to, graduation rates, retention rates, loan default rates and transfer rates.

Free Help Completing the FAFSA

For questions about federal student aid and help completing the FAFSA, call the Federal Student Aid Information Center at **1-800-4-FED-AID (1-800-433-3243)**. This is a toll-free hotline sponsored by the U.S. Department of Education. People living overseas or in other areas without access to toll-free numbers can call 1-319-337-5665. Hearing impaired individuals can call 1-800-730-8913.

Millions of people call 1-800-4-FED-AID each year. The most common questions asked are about getting help with completing the FAFSA, fixing PIN issues and checking the status of a student's FAFSA.

College Goal Sunday is another source of free help completing the FAFSA. College financial aid administrators volunteer to help families with the FAFSA on evenings and weekends in January, February and March each year. College Goal Sunday is sponsored by USA Funds and the Lumina Foundation. More information is available at www.collegegoalsundayusa.org.

Free help is also available from local college financial aid offices and high school guidance counselors.

There is also a help section on FAFSA on the Web (FOTW) with answers to common questions. Click on the question mark icon to access the Help section.

Finally, the Edvisors web site includes a lot of information and advice about completing the FAFSA at www.edvisors.com/fafsa/.

Step 2 – FAFSA ACCOUNT CREATION AND SETUP

Once students click on www.fafsa.ed.gov, they will be greeted with a student login screen as shown below.

Click on "Start a New FAFSA." This will show a page for creating a new account.

Start by entering the student's name, his or her Social Security Number and date of birth. When putting in numbers, do not use dashes, spaces, hyphens, periods, decimal points, commas, etc., as only digits are used with the FAFSA.

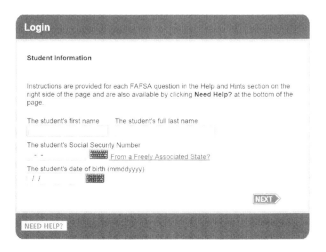

Notice the little keyboards next to some fields on the FAFSA. Clicking on this icon will pop up a virtual keyboard. The U.S. Department of Education added virtual keyboards to the FAFSA to help prevent identity theft. Instead of typing in some pieces of information on the FAFSA (especially on public computers at libraries, schools, etc.), the virtual keyboard uses the mouse to make it harder to steal that information through keystroke loggers.

Do students need to use it? If they are at a public computer, they might want to, but if they are at a home computer or using the computer of someone they trust, it's probably not necessary.

There's a dark blue border along the left hand side with the word, "STUDENT." This tells the student that the information he or she is currently completing is for the student. The border will change colors to purple and indicate "PARENT" when the form asks for parent information.

There are no age restrictions on eligibility for federal student aid. However, students who are under age 13 will not be able to use FAFSA on the Web (FOTW) because of the Children's Online Privacy Protection Act of 1998 (COPPA). COPPA precludes web sites from collecting personally identifiable information from underage children without verifiable parental consent. Instead, underage children will need to file a special paper version of the FAFSA that does not collect the student's email address. (Underage students may not communicate with the U.S. Department of Education by email.) This paper version of the FAFSA is available upon request by calling the Federal Student Aid Information Center at 1-800-4-FED-AID (1-800-433-3243) and asking for the COPPA-compliant version of the FAFSA.

After the student's initial login, the student may be asked which year's FAFSA he or she is completing. The FAFSA has an 18-month application cycle, from January 1 before the start of the award year to June 30 at the end of the award year. So, at times, there will be a choice of two consecutive award years, the current award year and the next award year. This can be a source of confusion. Students who are applying for financial aid for fall 2015 need to file a 2015-2016 FAFSA, not a 2014-2015 FAFSA. If the student submits a FAFSA for the wrong year, the student will need to submit a new FAFSA for the correct year. (If you are applying for summer 2015, ask the college financial aid administrator which form to file.)

The student may also be prompted as to whether he or she wishes to file a Renewal FAFSA or continue to complete a FAFSA that was started previously. (A Renewal FAFSA pre-fills the new FAFSA with some of the demographic

information from the previous year's FAFSA, reducing the time it takes to complete the FAFSA by about ten minutes.)

On the next screen, the applicant will be asked to create a password. The password should be between 4 and 8 characters long and may include numbers, uppercase letters and lowercase letters. Applicants should memorize or write down this password as they will need it later if they want to continue completing their FAFSA after taking a break.

If the applicant forgets his or her password, the password may be reset by clicking on the "I Forgot My Password" link. The form will ask for the student's permanent zip code before resetting the password. Otherwise, the student will need to call the Federal Student Aid Information Center at 1-800-4-FED-AID (1-800-433-3243) for help.

If the applicant is submitting a Renewal FAFSA, he or she will also be asked for his or her Federal Student Aid PIN at this time.

After students finish with the initial screen and click "Next," they will get the U.S. Department of Education's collection of FAFSA tips.

This section provides answers to commonly asked FAFSA questions.

Introduction Page - 2015-2016 FAFSA

Use the **Next** and **Previous** buttons to move from page to page in the form. If you use your browser's back and forward buttons to move from page to page, you may lose your data.

Additional information about *FAFSA on the Web*:

How can I get help completing my FAFSA?

How many steps does it take to complete?

How long will it take to complete?

Can I save my FAFSA if I can't finish it?

Documents needed to complete the FAFSA

Signing the FAFSA

FAFSA on the Web Security and Privacy

NEXT▷

EXIT

Students should click the "Next" button to continue to the actual FAFSA on the Web (FOTW).

Step 3 – COMPLETING THE FAFSA

Section 1 – Student Demographics

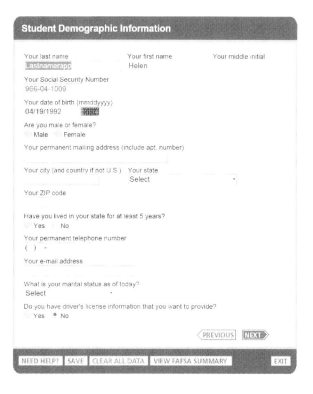

Once the student has created his or her FAFSA account, he or she will be asked to provide some basic demographic information. If the student has completed a FAFSA electronically in a previous year, these answers may be pre-filled. Double-check them and update the appropriate fields, as needed. If required, provide the Federal Student Aid PIN or username and password. Context-sensitive help is provided on the right-hand side of the screen as each question field is selected.

Student Name

It is important to list the student's name exactly as it is shown on the student's Social Security card. This is the student's legal name, not a nickname. FAFSA on the Web (FOTW) will ask for the student's last name, first name and middle initial. For example: report the first name as Susan, not Suzie, if Susan is the student's first name on the Social Security card.

If the student's name has changed because of marriage, divorce or a legal name change, the student should submit form SS-5, Application for a Social Security Card, to change the name with the Social Security Administration (SSA). However, since this can take some time (typically 10 days after SSA receives the application), it is best to complete the FAFSA with the name as it appears on the current Social Security card and update the Social Security Administration's records later.

Note that the last name is listed first, followed by the first name and middle initial. Some students accidentally list their first name first instead of second.

Student Social Security Number

Students and parents should refer to a copy of their actual Social Security cards to help ensure the correct number is reported. Transposing two digits in the Social Security Number (SSN) is a common mistake. Another mistake made by parents is to enter their own number or that of the student's sibling.

Both the student's name and Social Security Number must match the Social Security card exactly. The U.S. Department of Education conducts an electronic match of the student's name and Social Security Number with the Social Security Administration (SSA). A mismatch will cause the FAFSA to be rejected and may cause delays in the receipt of financial aid.

To apply for a Social Security Number (SSN) or to get a replacement

Social Security card, contact the Social Security Administration (SSA) at 1-800-772-1213 or TDD/TTY 1-800-325-0778 or visit their web site at: www.ssa.gov.

Although an error in the student's Social Security Number can be corrected on FAFSA on the Web (FOTW), the original incorrect Social Security Number may continue to be associated with the student's record as the record identifier, causing confusion. It may be better to submit a new original FAFSA with the correct Social Security Number. The student should ask the college's financial aid administrator whether to correct the original FAFSA or file a new FAFSA with the correct Social Security Number. The student should speak with the financial aid administrator before taking any action, as FOTW allows only one FAFSA to be associated with each Social Security Number.

If a student has a "work-only" Social Security Number (SSN) issued through the new Federal Deferred Action for Childhood Arrivals (DACA) policy or a Taxpayer Identification Number (TIN), the student is NOT eligible for federal financial aid. Students in this situation are encouraged to contact the colleges and universities they are considering to determine if state and/or institutional funds are available and, if so, what steps they should take to apply for such funding. Some colleges will ask DACA students to complete the FAFSA, even though they won't qualify for federal student aid, since they may qualify for state or institutional aid. (California DACA students, however, should complete the California Dream Act Application at www.caldreamact.org instead of the FAFSA.) If the financial aid administrator says to complete the FAFSA, select the "No, I am not a citizen or eligible noncitizen" answer to the question about citizenship status.

Students from the Freely Associated States (the Republic of Palau (PW), the Republic of the Marshall Islands (MH), or the Federated States of Micronesia (FM)) who do not have a Social Security Number should enter 666 for the first three digits of the Social Security Number. The federal processor will assign the remaining six digits when the FAFSA is processed. In subsequent years, these students from the Freely Associated

States must use the same pseudo-Social Security Number that was assigned to them previously.

Sometimes, the student will be a U.S. citizen or permanent resident and have a Social Security Number, but one or both of the student's parents will not have Social Security Numbers because they are not U.S. citizens or permanent residents. The student is still eligible for federal student aid and should complete the FAFSA with his or her Social Security Number. When the form asks for the parent's Social Security Numbers, enter 000-00-0000.

Permanent Mailing Address

The permanent mailing address is the same as the address the student uses on tax returns and voter registration cards. It is most likely NOT the student's address at school. For homeless students, parents, and families, or those living in transitional housing situations, this is an address where the student can receive postal mail, such as the address of a shelter or a PO Box. Students who do not have a permanent mailing address should ask the college's financial aid administrator for help.

If the student lives outside the United States, use 00000 as the zip code.

State of Legal Residence

The FAFSA asks for the student's state of legal residence. This is usually the state that the student lists as part of his or her permanent address, the student's home state. Do not use the student's campus mailing address. The student's FAFSA information will be provided to this state (as well as the state in which the student's college is located) to qualify him or her for state grants and other state aid.

The FAFSA asks the student for the date he or she became a legal resident of the state if he or she became a legal resident less than five years ago. (A similar question is asked of the parents, if the student is a dependent student.) Five years is used as a threshold because all states consider students who are U.S. citizens or eligible noncitizens to be residents of that state if they have lived there for at least five years.

States have varying criteria for determining whether or not the student is a resident for purposes of state financial aid and in-state tuition at public colleges. The state's flagship public college will usually have information about residency requirements on its web site. If the student is dependent, the state of legal residence is usually the state in which the custodial parents live.

Most states require the student (and the student's parent, if the student is a dependent student) to have been a state resident for at least 12 consecutive months (in some cases, a full calendar year) to qualify for in-state tuition. (Alaska requires 24 months and Arkansas requires 6 months. While Tennessee does not have a specific durational requirement, there must be clear and convincing evidence that the student and parents became state residents for reasons other than gaining eligibility for in-state tuition.) There are a variety of exceptions that vary by state. For example, some states allow children of active duty members of the military to qualify as state residents.

The state of legal residence is also used in the calculation of a student's financial aid eligibility by determining the appropriate allowance for state and other taxes paid by that state's residents.

Permanent Telephone Number

The permanent phone number can be a mobile/cell phone number as long as it is permanent enough that someone from a college financial aid office can call and reach the student. Don't use forwarded numbers, voice mail boxes, or the school's telephone number.

Email Address

Double-check the email address. Make sure there are no typos. The U.S. Department of Education and the colleges and universities to which the student is applying for financial aid will send FAFSA reminders, status updates, and application results to this email address.

Students may wish to create a new, professional-sounding email address for use with college admissions and financial aid applications. This email address must remain valid throughout the college admission and financial aid application period.

Student Marital Status

This question asks the student about his or her marital status as of the date the FAFSA is submitted. Note that this question is asking about the student's marital status, not the parents'.

If the student answers that he or she is currently married or remarried, the FAFSA will require information about the student's spouse. The spouse's income, tax and asset information must be combined with the student's information even if they got married after the end of the tax year. If the student checks that he or she has never been married, or is separated, divorced, or widowed, the FAFSA will not ask any questions about the student's spouse. (If the student is unmarried and a dependent student, the FAFSA will include questions for the student's parents.) This is an important question that can have a big impact on eligibility for financial aid.

Note that the student does not need to have a *legal* separation to be considered separated for federal student aid purposes. An *informal* separation will qualify, provided that the student and spouse do not live together. If the student and spouse live on separate floors of the same postal address, they are considered to be living together.

Marital status must be reported as of the date the FAFSA is submitted. Students should not anticipate a future change in marital status. If the student is married as of the date the FAFSA is filed, the FAFSA should be completed as married even if the student expects to get divorced or separated soon. Likewise, if a student expects to get married the day after filing the FAFSA, the student must complete the form as unmarried.

Due to the U.S. Supreme Court decision overturning the Defense of Marriage Act (DOMA), students who are in a same-sex marriage should identify themselves as married on the FAFSA if they were legally married in a state or foreign country that permits same-sex marriage, even if they currently live in a state that does not recognize same-sex marriage.[3]

A student who is married to a foreign national is still considered to be married. The student's spouse does not have to be a U.S. citizen.

Driver's License Number

If the student has a driver's license, enter the driver's license number and the state that issued it. If the student does not have a driver's license, leave these two questions blank. A driver's license is not required to apply for financial aid. Do not list a State ID Card number or conditional use permit number in these questions.

The student's driver's license number is used strictly for identity verification. A driver's license does not otherwise affect financial aid eligibility. It does not matter whether you have a good or bad driving record. Not having a driver's license will not affect aid eligibility, as another government-issued photo ID can be used for identity verification, such as a U.S. passport. The driver's license number is not used to verify citizenship or residency status or drug convictions.

Some colleges may use the student's driver's license as a way to verify that the student qualifies for institutional loans and grants that are restricted to state residents.

Note that many states require male students to have registered with Selective Service to obtain a new or renewal driver's license. These states include Alabama, Arizona, Arkansas, Colorado, Delaware, District of Columbia, Florida, Georgia, Hawaii, Idaho, Illinois, Indiana, Iowa, Kansas, Kentucky, Louisiana, Maine, Michigan, Minnesota, Mississippi, Missouri, Nevada, New Hampshire, New Mexico, New York, North Carolina, Ohio, Oklahoma, Rhode Island, South Carolina, South Dakota, Tennessee, Texas, Utah, Virginia, Washington, West Virginia and Wisconsin.

Citizenship Status

Students must be U.S. citizens or eligible noncitizens to receive federal student financial aid and state grants. If a student has recently become a U.S. citizen, he or she should contact the Social Security Administration (SSA) to ensure that his or her citizenship status is correctly associated with his or her Social Security Number. Otherwise, when the U.S. Department of Education matches data with the SSA, the SSA may report that the student is not a citizen and may be considered ineligible to receive federal and state aid.

For financial aid purposes, an eligible noncitizen is someone who meets one of the following criteria:

- A U.S. permanent resident with a Permanent Resident Card (I-551), also known as a green card

- A conditional permanent resident with a Conditional Green Card (I-551C)

- Other eligible noncitizen with an Arrival-Departure Record (I-94) from the Department of Homeland Security showing any of the following designations: *Refugee*, *Asylum Granted" Parolee* (I-94 confirms that the student was paroled for a minimum of one year and status has not expired), *T-Visa holder* (T-1, T-2, T-3, etc.) or *Cuban-Haitian Entrant*

- The holder of a valid certification or eligibility letter from the Department of Health and Human Services showing a designation of *Victim of human trafficking*

- A citizen of the Freely Associated States (i.e., the Republic of Palau (PW), the Republic of the Marshall Islands (MH), or the Federated States of Micronesia (FM))

- A Canadian-born Native American under terms of the Jay Treaty.

- Battered Immigrants-Qualified Aliens and their children, as provided for in the Violence Against Women Act.

Students who have received a notice of approval to apply for permanent residence (Forms I-171 or I-464) or family unit status (Form I-797) are not eligible for federal student aid. Students with temporary resident cards (Forms I-688, I-688A or I-688B) are also not eligible for federal student aid.

Eligible Noncitizen

If students indicate "eligible noncitizen," they should write in their 8- or 9-digit Alien Registration Number (ARN). Alien Registration Numbers may also be called A-Numbers. Students should precede an 8-digit number with a zero.

The U.S. Department of Education conducts an electronic match of the student's name and Alien Registration Number with the U.S. Department of Homeland Security. A mismatch will cause the FAFSA to be rejected and may cause delays in the receipt of financial aid.

Students who list their Alien Registration Number may be asked by the colleges or universities to provide a copy of their Permanent Registration Card.

Students who previously were an eligible noncitizen, but who are now U.S. citizens, should indicate their current citizenship status on the FAFSA. They should not provide an Alien Registration Number on the FAFSA.

Some recently naturalized citizens may also be asked to provide a copy of their Certificate of Naturalization. It is legal to photocopy the Certificate of Naturalization for financial aid purposes, despite notices to the contrary on the document.

Note that eligible noncitizens who are Battered Immigrants-Qualified Aliens or the child of a Battered Immigrant-Qualified Alien will fail the match of FAFSA data with the Department of Homeland Security (DHS) databases. The data of victims of domestic violence is not included in the DHS Systematic Alien Verification for Entitlements system to protect their privacy. College financial aid administrators may need to follow the instructions in Dear Colleague Letter GEN-10-07 to verify their eligibility.

Neither Citizen nor Eligible Noncitizen

If the student is not a U.S. citizen or eligible noncitizen, the student is not eligible for federal student aid. For example, students who are in the U.S. on an F-1 or F-2 student visa, a J-1 or J-2 exchange visitor visa, an M-1 vocational student visa, an A-1, A-2 or A-3 visa (foreign officials and their attendants), a B-1 or B-2 visitor visa (to work as a personal or domestic employee) or a G series visa (pertaining to international organizations) are not eligible for federal student aid.

Non-immigrant students who are in the U.S. on one of the following types of visas are not eligible for federal student aid: A, B, C, D, E, F, G, H, I, J, K, L, M, N, O, P, Q, R, S, TN, TD, V, TROV, and NATO.

However, some such students may be eligible for financial aid from their college or state and should check with the college as to which forms they should complete. Some colleges will ask the student to complete the FAFSA as a convenient way for the college to get the data they need to determine eligibility for need-based financial aid.

Note that T visa holders are eligible to apply for federal and some state student financial aid. T visa holders should file a FAFSA and identify themselves as eligible non-citizens.

U visa holders *are not* eligible for federal student financial aid, but they may be eligible for some state aid programs.

Family Unity Status individuals are not eligible for federal student financial aid.

A student with an I-94 stamped "Temporary Protected Status" is not eligible for federal student aid.

Selective Service Registration

Federal law requires that most male U.S. citizens (regardless of where they live) and male immigrants residing in the United States (permanent resident aliens), age 18-25, register with the Selective Service. Generally, any male student who is required to register with Selective Service must do so to receive federal student aid.

Exceptions to the Selective Service registration requirement include:

- Female students

- Male students who have not yet reached age 18

- Male students born in 1959 or an earlier year

- Male students enrolled in an officer procurement program at the Citadel (Charleston, SC), North Georgia College (Dahlonega, GA), Norwich University (Northfield, VT) or the Virginia Military Institute (Lexington, VA).

- Male students who are commissioned officers of the Public Health Service or a member of the Reserve of the Public Health Service who is on active duty[4]

Some states require Selective Service registration to enroll in a state college or university[5] or to qualify for state financial aid.[6] Some colleges and universities require Selective Service registration for the student to receive institutional financial aid funds.

Male students who have not yet registered with Selective Service may ask the U.S. Department of Education to register the student with Selective Service by checking the "Register me" box on the FAFSA. Only male students who are age 18 or older and who have not yet have turned age 26 as of the date the FAFSA is filed may register with Selective Service using the FAFSA. FAFSA on the Web (FOTW) will ask the student whether he wishes to register with Selective Service. (Female applicants will not be asked whether they want to be registered with Selective Service.)

Students who are male but age 17 or younger as of the date the FAFSA is submitted should leave the question blank. The student must register with Selective Service within 30 days of his 18th birthday. He can do this at the Selective Service web site, www.sss.gov, or fill out a Selective Service postcard at any U.S. post office.

If a student is unsure whether he has registered with Selective Service, he may check his registration status at www.sss.gov or call 1-888-655-1825 or 1-847-688-6888.

Transgender students must comply with the Selective Service registration requirement based on the student's gender at birth as listed on the student's birth certificate.[7] Thus, a student who was born male but underwent sex reassignment surgery to become female must register with Selective Service. Students who were born female but underwent sex reassignment surgery to become male are not required to register with Selective Service. (However, given the possibility of a data match conflict for students who are currently male, it may be advisable to register with Selective Service to avoid bureaucratic problems.)

Conscientious objectors are required to register with Selective Service. If a military draft is instituted, they will be able to file a claim for exemption based on religious or moral objections at that time.

Male students who are over age 26 but never registered with Selective Service may be ineligible for federal student aid and, possibly, also some state and institutional aid. They should first obtain a *status information letter* from Selective Service to determine whether or not they were required to register. If they were required to register but did not, they will need to provide the college financial aid administrator (not Selective Service) with a preponderance of evidence that the failure to register

was not *knowing and willful*. A preponderance of evidence means more evidence in favor than against. Examples include:

- Proof that the student did indeed register

- Proof that the student served full-time on active duty in the U.S. Armed Forces (e.g., a copy of the DD-214)

- Proof that the student attended one of the service academies (the U.S. Military Academy, the U.S. Naval Academy, the U.S. Air Force Academy, but not the Merchant Marine Academy)

- Proof that the student was hospitalized, institutionalized or incarcerated from age 18 to 25

- Proof that the student lived abroad from age 18 to 25

High School Completion Status

The student should indicate his or her High School Completion Status as of the beginning of the 2015-2016 school year.

Select the appropriate high school completion status[8]

- High school diploma (including foreign equivalents)

- GED certificate or state equivalent test (e.g., HiSET and TASC)

- Home schooled

Students who have not earned (or will not earn) a high school equivalency status, should select "None of the above."

Note that passing an ability-to-benefit test or completing 6 college credits is no longer a valid alternative to a high school diploma for students who first enroll in college on or after July 1, 2012.

Students who are still enrolled in an elementary or secondary school are not eligible for federal student aid funds. For example, students who are participating in dual enrollment programs, where the student is simultaneously enrolled in high school and an otherwise eligible college program, are not eligible for federal student aid. Students who are taking Advanced Placement (AP), International Baccalaureate (IB) or College-Level Examination Program (CLEP) classes are not eligible for federal student aid.

Grade Level

If the student is a senior in high school, he or she should indicate "Never attended college/1st year." The student should check this answer even if he or she has taken a college class while enrolled in high school.

The FAFSA is not limited to the first four years of postsecondary education. Students may file the FAFSA to apply for financial aid for the fifth year of an undergraduate degree program. Some forms of financial aid, however, are subject to limits that may affect the amount of financial aid available to a fifth year student.

- The cumulative loan limits for the Federal Stafford Loan are $31,000 for dependent undergraduate students and $57,500 for independent undergraduate students. The sum of the first four years annual loan limits are $27,000 and $45,000, respectively. That leaves $4,000 and $12,500 available for the fifth year if the student borrowed to the limit during the first four years.

- The Federal Pell Grant is subject to a lifetime eligibility limit (LEU) of the equivalent of 6 years of full-time enrollment.

- The American Opportunity Tax Credit is limited to the first four years of postsecondary education. Students may obtain the Lifetime Learning Tax Credit in the fifth and subsequent years.

Degree or Certificate Objective

The student should answer these questions for the school he or she is most likely to attend. The student should choose his or her most **immediate** degree objective even if he or she plans to seek an advanced degree (such as a law or medical degree) at a later date.

For example, if the student is planning to attend a community college for an Associate's degree in history leading to a transfer degree, he or she should select "Associate degree (general education or transfer program)." If the student is planning to attend a 4-year college in 2015-2016, select "1st bachelor's degree."

If the student is unsure of the type of school he or she will attend, select the "1st bachelor's degree."

Interest in Work-Study

This question tells the college whether the student is interested in receiving federal or college work-study funds.

Students who answer "Yes" to this question are not required to accept a work-study job. Students have the right to decline any forms of financial aid they do not want. Answering "Yes" also does not guarantee that the student will receive a college or Federal Work-Study job.

Please note that answering "No" to this question will not increase the amount of scholarship and grant aid a student will receive.

First Bachelor's Degree

This question asks students if they will have earned their first bachelor's degree before July 1, 2015.

Students who have already earned or completed the requirements for a Bachelor's degree are ineligible to receive certain forms of federal student aid, such as the Federal Pell Grant, Federal Supplemental Educational Opportunity Grant (FSEOG), and Teacher Education Assistance for College and Higher Education Grant (TEACH Grant). Students with a prior Bachelor's degree are still eligible for Federal Work-Study, Federal Perkins Loans, Federal Stafford Loans and Federal PLUS Loans.

Many private scholarships and state grant programs are also limited to the first Bachelor's degree.

Students who are double-majoring should be careful to avoid completing the requirements for either Bachelor's degree until the last academic term of their program. Otherwise, they may lose eligibility for some forms of financial aid after satisfying the requirements for the first Bachelor's degree.

Students who are enrolled in a post-baccalaureate program to obtain a teaching certificate or state license required for employment as an elementary or secondary school teacher are still considered undergraduate students for the TEACH and Federal Pell grant programs.

Students who will be pursuing a graduate (e.g., Master's or Ph.D.) or a professional degree (e.g., MD, JD, LLB or MBA) during 2015-2016 should answer "Yes" to this question even if they have not yet received a Bachelor's degree.[9]

Students who are enrolled in dual-degree programs that award a graduate or professional degree in addition to a Bachelor's degree are considered to be undergraduate students for at least the first three years of the program. Please consult with the college about how to complete this question in the fourth and subsequent years of the program.

Students who have received a Bachelor's degree from an unaccredited school, including a diploma mill, are ineligible for the Federal Pell Grant.

Students who have received a Bachelor's degree from a foreign school are ineligible for the Federal Pell Grant unless the student demonstrates to the financial aid administrator's satisfaction that the foreign degree is not the equivalent of a Bachelor's degree awarded by a U.S. college or university.

Parents' Educational Level

These questions are used for state grant purposes and do not affect eligibility for federal student aid. The answers to these questions are used to determine if the student is the first member of his or her family to attend college. Such a student is often called a "first-generation college student." Some states and colleges offer additional aid to students who are the first members of their family to go to college or graduate from college.

Select the highest grade level completed by the student's parents. Parent 1 and Parent 2 in these questions mean birth or adoptive parents, not legal guardians, stepparents, or foster parents. This differs from the definition of "parent" used in the rest of the FAFSA questions.

Please note that this question asks about the highest grade level *completed*, not the highest grade level *attended*. If a parent has attended college but not obtained a Bachelor's degree, the "High school" option should be marked.

Also, note that this is a screening question, defining college completion as having received a Bachelor's degree or more advanced degree. If a parent has obtained an Associate's degree or certificate but not a Bachelor's degree, the "High school" option should be marked because this parent has not completed a 4-year college degree program. Some states may have more restrictive definitions of first-generation college student status.

If a parent has completed the equivalent of a bachelor's degree or higher in a foreign country, he or she must select "College or beyond" even if the Bachelor's degree involved only three years of postsecondary education.

Student Aid Eligibility for Students with Drug Convictions

The purpose of this question is to determine whether the student has been convicted of possessing or selling illegal drugs while receiving federal student aid. Students who have a drug conviction should still complete the FAFSA. Some students with a drug conviction are ineligible for federal student aid for a period of time and some are not. Even if a student is ineligible for federal student aid, he or she may still be eligible for state and college student aid funds.

Students who have never attended college since high school will not be asked any of the drug conviction questions.

Students who indicate that they have attended college before will be asked if they have ever received federal student aid.

If they answer "Yes," they will be asked whether they have been convicted for the possession or sale of illegal drugs. Most students will answer "No" to this question and will not be asked any additional questions. Otherwise, the student will be asked to complete a worksheet that will ask about the number of convictions for selling or possessing illegal drugs and whether the student has completed an acceptable drug rehabilitation program since the student's conviction. Federal student aid will be suspended until the student completes the worksheet.

In short, according to the U.S. Department of Education, students should answer "No" if they have never received federal student aid or if they have never had a drug conviction for an offense that occurred while receiving federal student aid."

There are several types of convictions that do not cause the student to lose eligibility for federal student aid.

*   Convictions that did not occur during a period of college enrollment when the student was receiving federal student aid

*   Convictions that have been reversed or set aside

*   Convictions that occurred while the student was a minor, unless the student was tried as an adult

Students with these types of convictions should answer "No" to this question.

Students who were convicted of the possession or sale of illegal drugs while receiving federal student aid will have their eligibility suspended for a period of time. The duration of the suspension depends on the type of conviction and the number of previous offenses, as shown in this table:[10]

Suspension of eligibility	Possession of Illegal Drugs	Sale of Illegal Drugs
First offense	1 year from date of conviction	2 years from date of conviction
Second offense	2 years from date of conviction	Indefinite period
Third and subsequent offenses	Indefinite period	Indefinite period

Students who are convicted of both the possession and sale of illegal drugs will be ineligible for federal student aid and state aid for the longer of the two periods.

Students can regain eligibility before the end of the ineligibility period by successfully completing a qualified drug rehabilitation program or by passing two unannounced drug tests given by a qualified rehabilitation program.

High School Name and Location

In this question, students are asked to provide the name, city and state where they received, or will receive, their high school diploma. The students will then be asked to confirm that their high school is on the list that is displayed on FAFSA on the Web (FOTW). If the high school is not on the list, the student may type the name of the school. The FAFSA on the Web (FOTW) will not allow students who indicate that they have a high school diploma to skip this question.

The purpose of this question is to help high schools increase the number of students completing the FAFSA. The U.S. Department of Education will share this demographic (non-financial) information with the individual high schools attended by students who complete the FAFSA. The U.S. Department of Education will also compile and publish aggregate statistics by high school.

This question may also be used to verify that the student received a valid high school diploma from the listed high school.

Section 2 – School Selection

School Selection

You can add up to 10 colleges to your FAFSA. If you know your college's school code, use the option to the right to search. If you need help finding your college, use the state (required), city (optional), and school name (optional) fields to begin your search.

All of the information you report on the FAFSA will be sent to each college listed, including the names of the other colleges listed. If you don't want this information sent to a particular college, do not list that school on your FAFSA.

State Select

City ⁣ (optional)

School Name (optional)

Federal School Code

OR

SEARCH Search Tips

SEARCH

Select a school from the Search Results table and click Add >> to add a school to the Selected Schools table.

Search Results: 1

Sort By: Best Match | School Name

ALABAMA AGRCLTL & MECHL UNIV
NORMAL, AL
Federal School Code: 001002

Selected Schools

Select up to 10 schools

UNIVERSITY OF IOWA
IOWA CITY, IA
Federal School Code: 001892   Remove

UNIV OF ILLINOIS @ URBANA CHAMPAIGN
CHAMPAIGN, IL
Federal School Code: 001775   Remove

ALABAMA AGRCLTL & MECHL UNIV
NORMAL, AL
Federal School Code: 001002   Remove

ADD >>

VIEW SELECTED SCHOOL INFORMATION

PREVIOUS   NEXT

NEED HELP?   SAVE   CLEAR ALL DATA   VIEW FAFSA SUMMARY   EXIT

In Section 2 of the FAFSA, students may list up to ten schools to which they want their information sent. (The paper FAFSA allows only up to four schools.)

Financial aid is awarded by each individual college or university campus. Therefore, each campus to which the student is applying for financial aid must be listed separately in Section 2 of the FAFSA.

There are some additional features in this section of FAFSA on the Web (FOTW) that allow students to find more detailed information about each school, such as graduation rates and loan default rates.

Federal School Codes

Students will need a federal school code for each of the schools they list in Section 2. Students can look up their school codes when they are completing this section of FAFSA on the Web (FOTW). Entering the state where the school is located will make the search for the name of the college or university easier.

The city name is optional, but may help narrow the search. Generally, the city name is the city name that appears in the mailing address of the college, not the name of the local community. For example, the city name for the University of Pittsburgh is Pittsburgh, even though the University of Pittsburgh is located in the Oakland area.

The FAFSA on the Web (FOTW) recognizes many common abbreviations for school names, such as Caltech and MIT.

Federal school codes may also be found in the financial aid section of a college's web site.

Please note that the federal school code number is different from the code numbers used with the SAT, ACT and CSS/Financial Aid PROFILE. The Federal School Code begins with a letter or number (the number 0 or the letter G, B or E) followed by five digits.

The federal school code list is updated four times a year, in February, May, August and November.

Housing Plans

For each school, the student must select the housing plan that best describes the type of housing he or she expects to have while attending the school. There are three options:

- On campus

- With parent

- Off campus

The student should list "On campus" if he or she is unsure whether he or she will live with parents.

The student's choice of housing may affect the amount of financial aid for which he or she is eligible. It is usually more expensive to live on- or off-campus than with parents or relatives.

Please note that selecting the "On campus" housing option is not an application for on-campus housing. Ask each college or university about its application process for on-campus housing.

Applying for Financial Aid at More than Ten Schools

If students want to send their information to more than ten schools, they can delete and add schools when they receive their electronic Student Aid Report (SAR), SAR Acknowledgment or paper SAR. Receipt of the SAR is an indication that the colleges listed on the FAFSA have received their copy of the information submitted on the FAFSA. (The college's version of the SAR is called an Institutional Student Information Report (ISIR).)

Students can add, delete or change the listed schools by updating the information on FAFSA on the Web (FOTW). (Select "Make FAFSA Corrections" after logging in, then go to the "School Selection" page.)

Students can also change the list of colleges by calling the Federal Student Aid Information Center at 1-800-4-FED-AID (1-800-433-3243). The student will need to have his or her data release number (DRN) from the SAR when calling. Students can also add a school by giving their DRN to the school.

Do not confuse the DRN with the PIN. The PIN is used to file the FAFSA, access personal information on NSLDS and to sign the FAFSA and federal education loan promissory notes electronically. The PIN should not be shared with anybody. The DRN may be shared with college financial aid staff and the Federal Student Aid Information Center to allow them to access the information on the FAFSA.

Only the schools listed on the FAFSA will receive an ISIR for any subsequent updates or corrections in the student's information (and parent's information, if applicable). Colleges that were listed previously on the FAFSA can still get access to these changes, but will not be notified when a change occurs. The student should alert these colleges to changes in the student's data (or parent's data, if applicable).

Transferring to a Different College

Students who are transferring to a different college will need to add the new college to their FAFSA. Financial aid does not transfer with the student directly. Each college calculates the student's eligibility for student financial aid according to its own "packaging philosophy." Eligibility for federal aid may be affected by the student's degree level and enrollment status, as well as the amount of federal aid already used at the previous college during the current award year. For example, any previous federal student loan disbursements will be subtracted from the annual and cumulative loan limits. Note that some of the federal student aid used at the previous college may have to be returned to the federal government, depending on whether the student withdrew before reaching 60 percent of the way through the academic term. Since the regulations for return of Title IV federal student aid have a preference for returning loans before grants, this may affect the mix of loans and grants available to the student at the new college.

Does the Order in which Colleges are Listed Matter?

Each college or university must receive the student's information from the FAFSA before its financial aid deadline. So, if the student is applying to more than ten colleges and universities, the student should list the colleges and universities with the earliest financial aid deadlines in the first set of colleges and universities.

The order in which the ten colleges are listed also matters.[11] Colleges can see the full list of colleges listed on the FAFSA. Some colleges use this information as a form of competitive intelligence. Most students list the colleges in preference order. Research has shown that students are less likely to enroll at a college that appears further down the list. For example, while about half to two-thirds of students admitted by their first-choice college will enroll, only about ten percent will enroll at their third-choice college.

Some colleges want to maximize their *yield*, the percentage of admitted students who actually enroll at that school. Accordingly, some colleges are less likely to admit students who demonstrate less interest in the college. This is an open secret, although the practices at specific colleges are unknown. However, some private non-profit colleges may be more likely to use the student's preference order to influence college admissions decisions, since these colleges place more emphasis on improving their ranking in lists of top colleges.

Colleges also use the student's preference order to get more certainty about their incoming class. As more students apply to more colleges, not only are the students worried about whether they will get in, but the colleges also worry about whether the students will enroll.

The order in which colleges are listed on the FAFSA can also affect eligibility for financial aid. While the order does not affect eligibility for *federal* student aid, it can affect *state* and *institutional* aid. For example, the

U.S. Department of Education mentions the potential impact on state aid in its Guide to Completing the FAFSA:[12]

> *For purposes of federal student aid, it does not matter in what order you list the schools. However, to be considered for state aid, several states require you to list a state school first. Therefore, if you plan to list a state school in your state of residence as one of the schools in this section, you might want to list it first.*

Some colleges may use preferential packaging to award a smaller percentage of grants to students who list the college first, since students are more likely to enroll at their first-choice colleges even with a less favorable financial aid package.

So, what is the best order in which to list the colleges?

Listing the colleges in random or alphabetical order will not do any good, since the colleges will continue to assume that the first school in the list is the student's first choice. The aggregate statistics for the college's application pool demonstrate a strong correlation between the position of the college in the FAFSA's list of colleges and the chances the student will enroll if admitted. This allows a college to use FAFSA order to improve the college's yield by admitting only students who list the college in the first few positions on the FAFSA.

Listing one school at a time and waiting until receipt of the SAR to substitute the next school will not work, as every college listed on the FAFSA can see which colleges were listed previously and subsequently.

The first three positions matter most. The order of the colleges listed in the fourth through tenth positions generally will not have a big influence on college admissions and financial aid decisions.

One strategy that might work in the student's favor is to list his or her second-choice college first. The third-choice college should be listed in the second position and the first-choice college in the third position. A student's first-choice college is usually a long shot, where the student's preference for the college is unlikely to make a difference in the student's chances of admission. This is especially true of the most elite colleges that admit a very small percentage of the applicant pool. The student's second and third choices may be more reasonable options, where demonstrating a preference for the college may help influence the admission decision.

But it's not just the order of the schools that matters. It's also the set of schools. If a second-choice school sees several more elite institutions listed on the FAFSA and they believe, based on the student's admission application, that the student has a good chance of being admitted to one of those institutions, they might decide against admitting the student. After all, a student who gets into an Ivy League institution is unlikely to enroll at a second- or third-tier institution. So, this leads to strange circumstances where a student is admitted to an Ivy League institution and rejected by less selective institutions.

Note that after the student enters a list of schools on the FAFSA, he or she can change the order of the schools. It is only the final order of the schools, when the FAFSA is submitted, that is provided to the schools listed on the FAFSA.

If a college uses the colleges listed on the FAFSA and/or the order in which they are listed for college admissions decisions, the college is in violation of section 483(a)(3)(E) of the Higher Education Act of 1965 [20 U.S.C. 1090(a)(3)(E)]. The Higher Education Act prohibits using the information collected on the FAFSA for any purpose other than the "application, award and administration" of student financial aid. The U.S.

Department of Education is thinking about removing the list of colleges from the information provided to colleges. Any changes, however, will not occur until the 2016-2017 award year.

Need-Blind Admissions

A college is *need-blind* if it does not consider the family's finances when deciding whether to admit a student. Otherwise, the college is *need-sensitive* or *need-aware*.

Almost 100 colleges claim to have a need-blind admissions policy. Of these, only a third offer need-blind admissions to international students and four-fifths to transfer students. About a third will leave students with unmet need, leading to an "admit-deny" situation, where the college admits low-income students but denies them the financial aid they need to enroll.

Almost all need-blind schools become need-sensitive when admitting students off of the waiting list. Only five say that they are need-blind for wait-listed students: Amherst, Babson, Bard, Baylor and Wellesley.

Wealthy parents sometimes ask whether it is worthwhile to apply for financial aid, since applying for aid can affect whether a college will admit a student. Need-sensitive admissions can be a two-edged sword, since some colleges will admit wealthier students despite a marginal academic record. After all, the college will receive more net tuition revenue (and, possibly, future donations) from a high-income student than from a low-income student. Some colleges will even grant merit-based aid (more realistically, non-need-based aid) to attract such "full pay" students.

Families have a tendency to underestimate eligibility for need-based aid. So, unless the family can afford to pay for the full college costs with cash, it may be best for them to still apply for financial aid.

Some families skip applying for financial aid for the freshman year, figuring that they have enough resources to pay for the first year without financial aid and can apply for financial aid in subsequent years. Such a strategy can backfire, since some colleges will not award institutional aid to students who did not apply for financial aid the first year unless the family demonstrates a significant change in their financial circumstances. It does no good for the student to get into an expensive college if the student and his or her family can't afford the cost. The student will then be forced to drop out, transfer or graduate with excessive debt.

If the family is interested in only federal and state aid, they could wait until after the student is admitted to add the school to the student's FAFSA. A school can see the demographic and financial information from a student's FAFSA only if it is listed on the FAFSA.

Income Too High for Aid?

Some wealthy parents ask whether it is worthwhile to apply for financial aid if they earn a high income. They want to know what income and asset levels are too high to qualify for financial aid.

The FAFSA is a prerequisite for unsubsidized Federal Stafford and Federal PLUS loans. These loans are available without regard to demonstrated financial need. The family does not need to be poor to qualify for these federal education loans. Even wealthy students and parents can get these low-cost loans.

A student's demonstrated financial need is the difference between the college's cost of attendance (COA) and the student's expected family contribution (EFC). So, even a wealthy student might qualify for need-based aid at one of the more expensive colleges and universities.

The number of children in college may have a big impact on eligibility for need-based aid. Suppose a dependent student's parents earn $100,000 a year and have $250,000 in reportable assets. With one child in college, the EFC is about $29,000. That student might qualify for some need-based financial aid at an expensive private non-profit college that charges $50,000 or $60,000 a year, but not at a public college that charges half as much. However, with two children in college, each child's EFC might drop to $15,000, low enough that the children might qualify for need-based financial aid even at a public college.

On the other hand, 91.7% of Federal Pell Grant recipients in 2011-2012 had an adjusted gross income (AGI) under $50,000 and 99.8% had an AGI of $99,999 or less, based on data from the 2011-2012 National Postsecondary Student Aid Study (NPSAS). Among dependent students with only one family member in college, 94.1% of Pell Grant recipients had AGI under $50,000 and 99.8% had AGI of $99,999 or less.

Yet, some students whose parents earn six-figure salaries may still qualify for grants from the college. In 2011-2012, 11.3% of students whose parents earned $100,000 or more received need-based grants from their colleges and 18.9% received non-need and merit-based grants.

So, unless the parents earn more than $350,000 a year, have more than $1 million in reportable assets, have only one child in college and that child is enrolled at a public college, they should still file the FAFSA. If the family wants to receive federal education loans, they should file the FAFSA regardless of their income and assets.

Section 3 – Dependency Status

Dependency Determination

Were you born before January 1, 1992?
　Yes • No

As of today, are you married?
　Yes • No

At the beginning of the 2015-2016 school year, will you be working on a master's or doctorate program (such as an MA, MBA, MD, JD, PhD, EdD, or graduate certificate, etc.)?
　Yes • No

Do you now have or will you have children who will receive more than half of their support from you between July 1, 2015 and June 30, 2016?
　Yes • No

Do you have dependents (other than your children or spouse) who live with you and who receive more than half of their support from you, now and through June 30, 2016?
　Yes • No

Are you currently serving on active duty in the U.S. Armed Forces for purposes other than training?
　Yes • No

Are you a veteran of the U.S. Armed Forces?
　Yes • No

At any time since you turned age 13, were both your parents deceased, were you in foster care, or were you a dependent or ward of the court?
　Yes • No

As determined by a court in your state of legal residence, are you or were you an emancipated minor?
　Yes • No

As determined by a court in your state of legal residence, are you or were you in legal guardianship?
　Yes • No

On or after July 1, 2014, were you homeless or were you self-supporting and at risk of being homeless?
　Yes • No

⟨ PREVIOUS ⟩   NEXT

NEED HELP? SAVE CLEAR ALL DATA VIEW FAFSA SUMMARY   EXIT

The 13 questions in Section 3 are used to determine if the student is considered to be a *dependent* or *independent* student. Parent information is not required on the FAFSA of an independent student. This may increase the student's eligibility for need-based financial aid.

The definition of dependent on the FAFSA is not necessarily the same as the definition of dependent on federal income tax returns. Whether the parents list the student as a dependent (exemption) on their federal income tax return does not affect whether the student is considered a dependent for federal student aid purposes (or vice versa). The age thresholds, residency requirements and support tests all differ for the two definitions. A student could be financially self-sufficient and file his or her own income tax returns yet still be considered a dependent student for federal student aid purposes. (The two definitions are similar enough that significant discrepancies may cause the student's FAFSA to be selected for verification. For example, if a student is independent by virtue of having a dependent other than a spouse, but the student or the student's child is claimed as a dependent on his or her parents' federal income tax return, the college's financial aid administrator may question whether the student provided more than half of the child's support.)

Reaching the age of majority for the student's state of residence (age 18, 19 or 21) does not make a student independent. The FAFSA uses a higher age threshold.

The student will need to answer "Yes" or "No" to each of the questions in this section. The answers to some questions are pre-populated based on answers provided previously, such as the student's date of birth, marital status and level of education. If the student changes the answer to one of the pre-populated questions, FAFSA on the Web (FOTW) may require the student to resolve the discrepancy between this answer and the answer to the previous question.

If the student answers "No" to all of the questions in Section 3, the student will be considered a dependent student, even if the student is financially self-sufficient and does not live with his or her parents.

If the student answers "Yes" to one of the questions, the student will be considered to be an independent student. Skip-logic may cause some or all of the subsequent questions to be omitted, since they are no longer necessary to determine the student's dependency status. Only questions that serve a dual purpose, such as determining eligibility for military student aid, will remain.

Dependency Overrides

College financial aid administrators have the authority, on a case-by-case basis, to override a student's dependency status from dependent to independent in unusual circumstances, including, but not limited to, incarceration, hospitalization, institutionalization or incapacitation of both parents, voluntary or involuntary removal of the student from the parent's home due to an abusive family situation that threatens the student's health and/or safety, court protection from abuse orders against the parents or abandonment (parent whereabouts unknown). For example, if the student's parents are divorced and the custodial parent dies, normally the noncustodial parent would become responsible for completing the FAFSA. But, sometimes the student has not had any contact or support from this parent for a long time and the parent's whereabouts are unknown. In such a situation, the college financial aid administrator might decide to treat an otherwise dependent student as an independent student.

The definition of abandonment is subjective, but generally involves a lack of support or contact for an extended period of time, typically at least a year, and an inability to locate the parents. For example, if the student's custodial parent dies and the student has had no contact or financial support from the noncustodial parent for a decade, many financial aid administrators will justify a dependency override based on abandonment.

None of the following circumstances are sufficient justification, even in combination, for a college financial aid administrator to perform a dependency override:

- A student cannot qualify as an independent student because the student's parents did not claim the student as a dependent on their federal income tax return, not even if the student demonstrates total financial self-sufficiency.

- A student cannot qualify as an independent student because the student's parents refuse to contribute to the student's education.

59

- A student cannot qualify as an independent student because the student's parents refuse to provide information on the FAFSA.

- A student cannot qualify as an independent student because the student's parents refuse to participate in the financial aid verification process.

- A student cannot qualify as an independent student because the student's parents live in another country.[13]

A dependency override is in only one direction, from dependent to independent. College financial aid administrators cannot treat a student who satisfies the statutory requirements for independent student status as though the student is dependent.

To request a dependency override, send a letter to the college's financial aid administrator asking for a dependency override. Summarize the circumstances that justify the dependency override. Provide copies of independent third-party documentation of the special circumstances, such as letters from social workers, clergy, teachers, guidance counselors, doctors or others who are familiar with the student's situation.

Please note that the decision of the college financial aid administrator is final and cannot be appealed.

Dependency overrides are for one year at a time. Financial aid administrators must verify that the unusual circumstances that justified the dependency override in a previous year continue to apply.

The 13 Dependency Status Questions

Were you born before January 1, 1992?

Students who will reach age 24 by December 31 of the award year are considered to be automatically independent. This question is asking whether the student was born in 1991, 1990 or an earlier year. Students who were born *on* January 1, 1992 should answer "No" to this question, even though they missed the cut-off by a single day.

As of today, are you married?

The student should answer this question about the student's marital status as of the date the FAFSA is filed. Students who are married are considered to be automatically independent.

This question concerns the student's marital status, not the parent's marital status.

Criteria for Independent Student Status

A student is considered to be independent if he or she satisfies any of these criteria:

- Age 24 as of December 31 of award year
- Married
- Dependent children
- Dependents other than a spouse
- Graduate or professional school student
- Veteran or active duty member of the U.S. Armed Forces
- Orphan, foster child or ward of the court
- Emancipated minor
- Legal guardianship
- Unaccompanied youth who is homeless or unaccompanied youth who is self-supporting and at risk of being homeless
- Dependency override

Students should not anticipate a future change in marital status. For example, if the student plans to get married the day after filing the FAFSA, the student should list his or her marital status as unmarried. A student who is engaged is not considered to be married. College financial aid administrators can ask for a copy of the student's marriage certificate, divorce decree or separation agreement to verify the answer to this question.

A student who is separated is considered to still be married and should answer "Yes" to this question.

A student who satisfied the criteria for common-law marriage in the student's state of residence should answer "Yes" to this question. Only 15 states recognize common-law marriage. Generally, to be considered married under a common-law marriage, the couple must intend to be married, cohabit (live together), hold themselves out as married (e.g., using the same last name, filing joint federal income tax returns, maintaining a joint bank account, referring to each other as husband and wife), have a reputation in the community as married and live together for a significant amount of time. The couple must also have the legal and mental capacity to be married (e.g., neither spouse married to someone else, both over the legal age to be married). Specific criteria for a common-law marriage vary from state to state. Students who satisfy the criteria for a common-law marriage and move to a state that does not recognize common-law marriages are still considered to be married.

Common-Law Marriage States

- Alabama
- Colorado
- District of Columbia
- Georgia (if created before 1/1/1997)
- Idaho (if created before 1/1/1996)
- Iowa
- Kansas (both age 18 or older)
- Montana
- Ohio (if created before 10/10/1991)
- Oklahoma (if created before 11/1/1998)
- Pennsylvania (if created before 1/1/2005)
- Rhode Island
- South Carolina
- Texas ("informal marriage")
- Utah (only if validated by court/administrative order)

A student who is in a same-sex marriage (legally married in a state or country that recognizes same-sex marriages) is considered to be married for federal student aid purposes and should answer "Yes" to this question, even if the student currently lives in a state that does not recognize same-sex marriage. (On June 26, 2013, the U.S. Supreme Court ruled that Section 3 of the Defense of Marriage Act (DOMA) is unconstitutional.)

The student's marital status cannot be changed mid-year except in very limited circumstances. If a student expects his or her marital status to change, the student may wish to delay filing the FAFSA until after the change in status. However, students should not delay filing the FAFSA if they live in one of the states that awards state grants on a first-come, first-served basis or if the delay will cause the student to miss a state or institutional financial aid deadline.

Since July 1, 2012, college financial aid administrators may require a student to update the student's marital status (and, consequently, the student's household size, number in college and dependency status) "to address an inequity or to more accurately reflect the applicant's ability to pay."[14] Note that college financial aid administrators are permitted to update the student's marital status but are not required to do so. A college may establish "a cut-off date after which it will not consider any updates to a student's marital status." A financial aid administrator might allow a change in the student's marital status due to the death of a spouse, divorce or separation due to a court protection from abuse order against the spouse, or divorce or separation due to incarceration or incapacitation of the spouse. These circumstances yield a significant change in the student's ability to pay. It may also be difficult or dangerous for the

States with Early FAFSA Deadlines

First-come, First-served (9)
- Illinois
- Kentucky
- North Carolina
- South Carolina
- Tennessee
- Texas
- Vermont
- Washington (state)
- Washington, D.C.

February Deadlines (3)
- Connecticut
- Oregon
- Utah

March Deadlines (11)
- California
- Hawaii
- Idaho
- Indiana
- Maryland
- Michigan
- Mississippi
- Montana
- Oklahoma
- Rhode Island
- West Virginia

student to comply with requests to obtain or verify the spouse's financial information in such circumstances.

Are you a graduate or professional school student?

The full question is: "At the beginning of the 2015-2016 school year, will you be working on a master's or doctorate program (such as an MA, MBA, MD, JD, PhD, EdD, graduate certificate, etc.)?"

Students who are enrolled or will be enrolled in graduate or professional school at the start of the academic year are considered to be automatically independent and should answer "Yes" to this question. This includes students enrolled in a Master's degree or doctoral program, as well as students pursuing an M.D., L.L.B., J.D. or other professional degree.

A student who will still be enrolled in an undergraduate degree program at the start of the academic year should answer "No" to this question. After the student has completed the undergraduate degree program and started the graduate or professional degree program, the student can update the FAFSA and have his or her expected family contribution (EFC) recalculated. The college's financial aid administrator can adjust the student's status on the FAFSA.

The change in grade level will make the student eligible for the higher federal loan limits available to graduate and professional students in the Federal Stafford and Federal Perkins loan programs. It may also make the student eligible for the Federal Grad PLUS loan. However, graduate and professional students are not eligible for the Federal Pell Grant, so a student who incorrectly answers "Yes" to this question will need to correct the answer to regain his or her potential eligibility for the Federal Pell Grant.

Are you an active-duty member of the U.S. Armed Forces?

The full question is: "Are you currently serving on active duty in the U.S. Armed Forces for purposes other than training?"

Students who are currently serving in the U.S. Armed Forces on active duty for other than training purposes are considered to be independent students. The U.S. Armed Forces include the Army, Navy, Air Force, Marines and Coast Guard.

A member of the National Guard or Reserves may answer "Yes" to this question if he or she is on active duty for other than state or training purposes. The student must be on active *federal* duty by presidential order to qualify as an independent student. If the student is on active duty for state service or for training purposes, he or she must answer "No" to this question.

Are you a veteran of the U.S. Armed Forces?
Veterans are automatically independent.

To be considered a veteran for federal student aid purposes, the student must have served at least one day on active duty (including basic training) and have been released under a condition other than dishonorable. Note that veteran status for federal student aid purposes is different from veteran status for Department of Veterans Affairs (VA) benefits.

The following types of service qualify:

- Service in the U.S. Armed Forces qualifies.

- Service in National Guard or Reserves qualifies only if the student was called up to active duty *federal* service by a presidential order for a purpose other than training. State service does not qualify.

- Students who attended a U.S. service academy or preparatory school for at least one day. These include the U.S. Military Academy, U.S. Naval Academy, U.S. Air Force Academy, U.S. Coast Guard Academy, U.S. Merchant Marine Academy, U.S. Military Academy Preparatory School, U.S. Naval Academy Preparatory School and the U.S. Air Force Academy Preparatory School.

A student who is not yet a veteran but will be by the end of the award year should answer "Yes" to this question. Students who are currently attending a U.S. service academy or preparatory school but who have not yet been discharged should answer "No" to this question.

Students serving in ROTC are not considered veterans.

If the student indicates that he or she is a veteran, the U.S. Department of Education will conduct a match of the student's name, date of birth and other identifiers against the Department of Veterans Affairs (VA) records. If the student fails the data match, the student will need to provide the college financial aid administrator with a copy of the student's DD-214 (Certificate of Release or Discharge from Active Duty). The "Character of Service" on the DD-214 should show anything other than "Dishonorable." See box for additional details. A letter from a superior officer can also suffice, if the letter documents the same sort of information that would appear on a DD-214, such as the nature of the call to active duty service and the character of service. If there is an error in the VA's records, the student should contact the VA to get the records corrected.

Character of Service (Box 24 of DD-214)

The requirement that the student have been released under a condition other than dishonorable can be confusing, since one of the six possible discharge statuses is "Under Other Than Honorable Conditions." A student with that status is still considered to be a veteran for federal student aid purposes. Only students who have a character of service of "dishonorable" are not considered to be a veteran for federal student aid purposes.

The six possible values for the character of service are as follows:
- Honorable
- Under Honorable Conditions (General)
- Under Other Than Honorable Conditions
- Bad Conduct
- Dishonorable
- Uncharacterized

Do you have children or other legal dependents?

The FAFSA has two similar questions, one about children of the student and the other about legal dependents of the student:

- "Do you now have or will you have children who will receive more than half of their support from you between July 1, 2015 and June 30, 2016?"

- "Do you have dependents (other than your children or spouse) who live with you and who receive more than half of their support from you, now and through June 30, 2016?"

If the student has children or legal dependents other than a spouse, the student is considered to be independent.

For the student's child to qualify the student for independent student status, the child must satisfy one criterion:

- The child must receive more than half of his or her support during the award year (from July 1, 2015 through June 30, 2016).

The child is *not* required to live with the student. Unborn children count so long as they will be born before the end of the award year and will receive more than half their support from the student. Some colleges may require a letter from a doctor to document the pregnancy.

For a legal dependent other than a spouse to qualify the student for independent student status, the dependent must satisfy three criteria:

- The dependent must receive more than half of his or her support from the student

- The dependent must continue to receive more than half of his or her support through the end of the award year (June 30, 2016)

- The dependent must live with the student

A key difference between dependent children and legal dependents other than a spouse is the requirement that a legal dependent, but not a child, must live with the student for the student to count him or her in the student's household size and for the student to qualify as an independent student.

Please note that a spouse is excluded from the definition of legal dependent because being married is sufficient for the student to be considered independent. The student does not have to support or live with his or her spouse to be considered independent.

Support is measured against the full year. If the student starts supporting the child mid-year, the support provided for the remainder of the year must be more than half of the child's support for the entire year.

Support includes direct financial support, such as money, gifts and loans. It also includes food, clothing, housing, transportation (e.g., car payments, insurance, fuel and maintenance), medical and dental care and insurance, and college costs. It also includes indirect financial support, such as money paid to a third party to pay for expenses for which the student is responsible, such as cell phone, auto insurance and cable TV payments.

Whether the *student* provides more than half the child's support is measured by comparing support received directly or indirectly from the *student's parents* against support provided by other sources. The student can count as part of his or her support of the child amounts received from any source other than his or her parents, such as child support and government assistance programs (e.g., TANF, SNAP), not just income earned by the student. Money provided by the student's parents to the student does *not* count as part of the student's support of the child.

If the student is living with his or her parents, in most cases, the student's parents will be providing more than half of the support for the student's child, since food and housing count for a large portion of the child's support.

This can lead to counterintuitive results where a child's mother and father are each counted as providing more than half of the child's support. The child's mother gets to count child support received from the child's father as part of her support of the child on her FAFSA, since the money did not come from her parents. If the child support represents more than half of the child's support, the child's father can count the child in household size on his FAFSA. Then, both the child's mother and father will be considered independent by virtue of providing more than half of the child's support. The child does not need to live with either parent to be counted in his or her household size or for each parent to be considered independent by virtue of having a dependent other than a spouse.

Are you an orphan, foster child or ward of the court?

The full question is: "At any time since you turned age 13, were both your parents deceased, were you in foster care, or were you a dependent or ward of the court?"

An orphan is a child whose biological and/or adoptive parents are both dead. If a student becomes an orphan when he or she is age 13 or older, the student is considered to be an independent student, even if the student is subsequently adopted. If the student was adopted prior to reaching age 13, he or she is not considered to be an orphan for federal student aid purposes.

A child who is in foster care is placed in a substitute home (including the private home of a foster parent or a group home) because of neglect, abandonment or abuse. If a student is in foster care when the student is age 13 or older, the student is considered to be an independent student, even if the student is no longer in foster care on the date the FAFSA is filed.

A student becomes a ward of the court when the court has taken legal custody of the student (e.g., the student is a dependent of the court). If a student is a ward of the court when the student is age 13 or older, the student is considered to be an independent student. Please note that a student who is incarcerated is not considered to be a ward of the court. If the student remains in the legal custody of his or her parents, the student is not considered to be a ward of the court.

Because of the potential for confusion, college financial aid administrators may ask the student for proof that the student is/was a ward of the court, such as a copy of the court order. The financial aid administrator may seek clarification from the court. It may be helpful to ask the court whether the student qualifies under the specific legal citation, 20 USC 1087vv(d)(1)(B).

Orphans and wards of the court are less likely to enroll in and graduate from college. Based on data from the 2009 follow-up to the 2003-2004 Beginning Postsecondary Students longitudinal study (BPS:04/09), about a third of students who were orphans or wards of the court under age 24 in 2003-2004 graduated from college by 2009, compared with about half of other undergraduate students.

Are you an emancipated minor?

The full question is: "Are you or were you an emancipated minor as determined by a court in your state of legal residence?"

An emancipated minor is a student who was released from legal custody of his or her parents prior to reaching the age of majority by court order. Please note that the court must have been located in the student's state of legal residence at the time the order was issued. An emancipated minor is considered to be an independent student.

While the term "emancipation" is often used in connection with the end of child support obligations when the student's parents are divorced, such a student is not considered to be an emancipated *minor*. Emancipation for child support purposes occurs when the child reaches the age of majority (typically age 18, 19 or 21), while an emancipated minor becomes an adult *before* reaching the age of majority.

Because of the potential for confusion, college financial aid administrators may ask the student for proof that the student is an emancipated minor, such as a copy of the court order.

Are you or were you in a legal guardianship?

The full question is: "Are you or were you in legal guardianship as determined by a court in your state of legal residence?"

A student who is in a legal guardianship, as determined by a court of competent jurisdiction, is considered to be an independent student. Please note that the court must have been located in the student's state of legal residence at the time the order was issued. The legal guardianship must have been established by court order. A legal guardianship established by an attorney is not sufficient.

Note that court-ordered legal guardianships are not available in all states. Some states, like Virginia, provide only legal custody as an option. Legal custody is not considered to be the same as legal guardianship for federal student aid purposes.

Students who are in a legal guardianship with their parents as guardians, such as an adult disabled student in his or her parent's care, are not considered to be independent and should answer "No" to this question.

A temporary legal guardianship does not count if the legal guardianship is no longer in effect or was not in effect at the time the student reached the age of majority.

Because of the potential for confusion, college financial aid administrators may ask the student for proof that the student is or was in a legal guardianship, such as a copy of the court order.

Are you an unaccompanied homeless youth?

There are three related questions that are used to determine whether the student is considered to be an unaccompanied homeless youth:

- "At any time on or after July 1, 2014, did your high school or school district homeless liaison determine that you were an unaccompanied youth who was homeless or were self-supporting and at risk of being homeless?"

- "At any time on or after July 1, 2014, did the director of an emergency shelter or transitional housing program funded by the U.S. Department of Housing and Urban Development determine that you were an unaccompanied youth who was homeless or were self-supporting and at risk of being homeless?"

- "At any time on or after July 1, 2014, did the director of a runaway or homeless youth basic center or transitional living program determine that you were an unaccompanied youth who was homeless or were self-supporting and at risk of being homeless?"

An unaccompanied homeless youth is considered to be an independent student, as is an unaccompanied youth who is self-supporting and at risk of being homeless.

A student may be determined to have this status by his or her high school or school district's homeless liaison, the director of an emergency shelter or transitional housing program, or by the director of a runaway or homeless youth basic center or transitional living program.

College financial aid administrators may also determine that a student is an unaccompanied homeless youth or an unaccompanied youth who is self-supporting and at risk of being homeless.

The definitions of unaccompanied youth and homeless follow the definitions from the McKinney-Vento Homeless Assistance Act of 1987 (P.L. 100-77).[15]

- A **youth** is 21 years old or younger or still enrolled in high school as of the date the FAFSA is filed.

- A student is **unaccompanied** if he or she is not living in the physical custody of his or her parent or legal guardian.

- A student is **homeless** if he or she does not have "fixed, regular and adequate nighttime residence."[16] This includes a student who is temporarily living with other people, such as a friend's parents, because the student has nowhere else to go. It also includes students who live in a homeless shelter, in a car, in a hotel/motel, in a park, in an abandoned building, bus or train station, airport, substandard housing, camp ground, or any "public or private place not designed for or ordinarily used as sleeping accommodation for human beings".[17]

Students who have run away from an abusive parent may also qualify, even if the parent would support the student and provide the student with housing. Students who have been kicked out of their parents' home also qualify.

The National Association for the Education of Homeless Children and Youth (NAEHCY) provides a form that may be used to obtain a determination that the student is an unaccompanied homeless youth or an unaccompanied youth who is self-supporting and at risk of homelessness.

To answer "Yes" to these questions, the student must have a determination as an unaccompanied homeless youth or as an unaccompanied youth who is self-supporting and at risk of being homeless. Such a determination is provided only to students who are in high school or who are receiving services from these programs. Students who do not have such a determination but who feel that they satisfy the definition should ask the college's financial aid administrator to make such a determination. The financial aid administrator also has the option of performing a dependency override if he or she decides that the student's circumstances merit an override.

Otherwise, a student should answer "No" if he or she is not homeless; is not self-supporting or is not at risk of being homeless; and does not have a determination from a district liaison, director of a cited program, or the college's financial aid administrator.

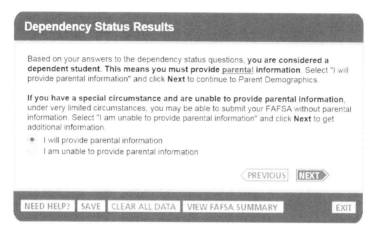

What's Next

Once the student has completed the dependency questions in Section 3, the FAFSA will determine whether or not the student is considered a dependent student. Students who answer "No" to every question in Section 3 are considered to be dependent. Students who answer "Yes" to any of the 13 questions in Section 3 are considered to be independent.

Students who are dependent must have their parents complete the parent section of the FAFSA and should continue with Section 4 of the FAFSA. Students who are independent are not required to complete the parent section of the FAFSA and should skip to Section 5 of the FAFSA.

Please note that some professional schools (e.g., medical and law schools) will require students to complete Section 4 of the FAFSA even though the student is considered an independent student. Answering these questions will not affect eligibility for federal or state aid. However, it provides the school with the data to use in determining the student's eligibility for institutional financial aid funds. It is not uncommon for some law and medical schools to require this information for students up to age 26, 28 or even 30, even if the student is married. Generally, the parent will not be required to sign the FAFSA for these applicants, since the parent's information is not required for federal student aid eligibility.

Special Circumstances and Independent Student Status

If students feel that they have special circumstances that should qualify them as an independent student even though they technically fall under the dependent student classification, the FAFSA on the Web (FOTW) provides a mechanism for students to complete the FAFSA without providing parental information.

If the student is classified as a dependent student, but cannot provide parental information, he or she should select "I am unable to provide parental information" and click the "Next" button. The FAFSA will then ask the student if he or she has a special circumstance that might qualify him or her to file as an independent student.

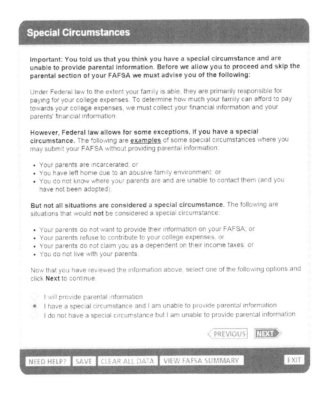

If the student has a special circumstance, he or she should select the appropriate response. The FAFSA will then allow the student to submit the FAFSA without completing the parental information questions. Special circumstances include, but are not limited to, situations in which the student's parents are incarcerated, the whereabouts of the student's parents are unknown, or the student left home because of an abusive family environment.

Please note that the final determination of whether a student qualifies for a dependency override is made by the college's financial aid administrator. Indicating that the student has a special circumstance on the FAFSA is not sufficient. It merely provides a mechanism for the student to complete the FAFSA when the student does not have access to parental information. Appeals are considered on a case-by-case basis and are decided by each individual college. Not all appeals will be granted.

Unable to Provide Parental Information

You told us that you are unable to provide parental information.

Review the following to continue.

1. We will allow you to submit your FAFSA without parental information, however **your FAFSA will not be considered complete**.
2. Because your FAFSA is not considered complete, we **will not calculate your Expected Family Contribution (EFC)**, which is the index used by colleges to determine how much student aid you are eligible to receive.
3. If you are approaching any deadlines for your state, college, or scholarship aid, you may want to contact your financial aid administrator **before** submitting your FAFSA without parental data.
4. Once you submit your FAFSA without parental data, <u>you must follow up with the financial aid administrator at the college you plan to attend</u>, in order to complete your FAFSA and receive an EFC. Also, note the following:

- Under Federal law, only your financial aid administrator has the authority to decide whether or not you must provide parental information on your FAFSA.

- You will have to provide documentation to verify your situation. Gather as much written evidence of your situation as you can. Written evidence may include court or law enforcement documents, letters from a clergy member, school counselor or social worker, and/or any other relevant data that explains your special circumstance.

- After reviewing your circumstances carefully, **your financial aid administrator will decide** if you must provide parental information or if your circumstances allow you to proceed without providing parental data. **Your financial aid administrator's decision is final** and cannot be appealed to Federal Student Aid.

Select one of the following options and click **Next** to continue.
- I will provide parental information
- I am unable to provide parental information and acknowledge that my FAFSA will be submitted without calculating an EFC

< PREVIOUS | NEXT >

| NEED HELP? | SAVE | CLEAR ALL DATA | VIEW FAFSA SUMMARY | EXIT |

If the student does not have a special circumstance, but is unable to provide parental information, FAFSA on the Web (FOTW) will allow the student to complete the form without parental information if the student selects the second option. However, a dependent student who does not provide parental information will not qualify for federal student aid. (The student might still be eligible for state aid or financial aid from the school.)

If the student does not qualify for a dependency override but is unable to provide parental information because the student's parents refuse to complete the form and have cut off all financial support, the college's financial aid administrator can allow the student to borrow from the unsubsidized Federal Stafford loan program. Such a student, however, is not eligible for other forms of federal student aid, such as the Federal Pell Grant, Federal Supplemental Educational Opportunity Grant (FSEOG), Federal Perkins Loan, subsidized Federal Stafford Loan and Federal Work-Study.

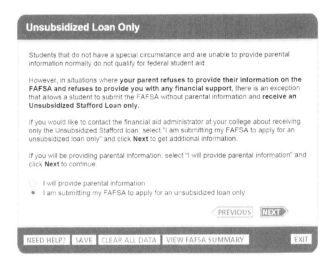

Section 4 – Parent Demographics

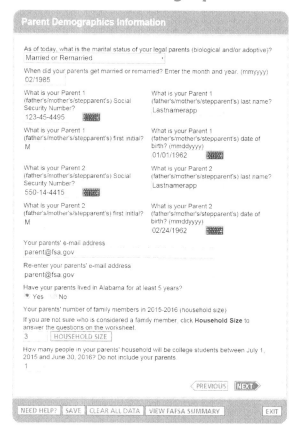

This section asks questions about the parent(s) whose information is required on FAFSA on the Web (FOTW). The student's parents must provide answers to the questions in Sections 4 and 5 if the student is a dependent student (i.e., if he or she answered "No" to every question in Section 3). The Expected Family Contribution (EFC) calculation, determined by a congressional formula, uses information from this part of the FAFSA to determine what portion of the student's parents' income and assets should be available to contribute to the student's educational cost of attendance in the 2015-2016 academic year. Students should answer all of the questions in Sections 4 and 5 even if they do not live with their legal parents (e.g., their biological and/or adoptive parents).

Remember, if the parents whose information is reported on the FAFSA have not yet completed their 2014 federal income tax forms, it is important that they use the best estimates of their total 2014 taxable and untaxed income. W-2s, final 2014 paycheck stubs, or any other employment or taxableincome records may help parents to estimate. It is OK to use estimated 2014 income information when completing the FAFSA.

Tips for Answering Financial Questions

If the answer to any question is zero, or the question does not apply, enter the number 0. Do not leave any question blank.

Always report whole dollar figures (rounding to the nearest dollar); ignore any cents. Do not use commas, decimal points or dashes when reporting numbers.

Parents and students who use estimated income figures will be required to correct the estimated income amounts when they have filed their actual federal tax returns or other documentation becomes available.

Who is Considered a Parent?

It is important to determine who is considered a parent on the FAFSA. Students and their parents must answer all the questions in Section 4 as of the date they complete and submit FAFSA on the Web (FOTW).

For federal student aid purposes, a student's parents are not limited to just biological parents. An adoptive parent is treated in the same manner as a biological parent on the FAFSA. For example, if the student's grandparent legally adopts the student, the grandparent will be required to complete the FAFSA. But, if the grandparent is a legal guardian for the student and has not adopted the student, the grandparent cannot substitute for the parents on the FAFSA, even if the student is living with the grandparent. (If the grandparents have not adopted the student, any support provided by the grandparents must be reported as untaxed income to the student on the FAFSA, regardless of the student's dependency status.)

A student's legal parents can also include a parent who was listed on the student's birth certificate, even if this parent is not a biological or adoptive parent.

If the student's biological or adoptive parents are both living and married to each other, select "Married or Remarried" and provide information about both of them, regardless of their gender. Consistent with the 2013 U.S. Supreme Court decision on the Defense of Marriage Act (DOMA), same-sex couples must report their marital status as married if they were legally married in a state or country that permits same-sex marriage, even if they currently live in a state that does not recognize same-sex marriage.

If a student has two same-sex parents, one biological or adoptive and one not, and the biological or adoptive parent dies, the surviving parent is treated the same as a surviving stepparent, since this person's status as a parent was derived through his or her relationship to the biological or adoptive parent, not through his or her relationship to the student. The surviving same-sex parent would have to be a biological or adoptive parent or listed as a parent on the student's birth certificate to continue being considered a parent for federal student aid purposes.

If the student's legal parents (e.g., biological and/or adoptive parents) are not married to each other and live together, select "Unmarried and both parents living together" and provide information about both of them, regardless of their gender. This includes a student whose parents were never married but live together, as well as

Definition of Custodial Parent

1. The parent with whom student lived the most during the 12 months preceding the FAFSA submission date.
2. Otherwise, the parent who provided more financial support to the student during the 12 months preceding the FAFSA application date.
3. Otherwise, the parent who provided more financial support to the student during the most recent calendar year for which parental support was provided.

a student whose parents are divorced or separated but living together. Do not, however, base the marital status on any person who is not the student's legal parent and who is not married to the student's parent.

Separation can include either a legal separation or an informal separation. Parents with an informal separation cannot live together. If the student's parents had an informal separation and are now living together, they are no longer considered as having a separation and should check "Married or Remarried" instead. According to the U.S. Department of Education, "When two married persons live as a married couple but are separated by physical distance (or have separate households), they are considered married for FAFSA purposes." If one of the parents lives in a different state for his or her job, but otherwise the marriage is intact, the parents are not considered to be separated on the FAFSA.

Starting with the 2014-2015 award year, parents who are divorced or separated but living together are treated the same as married parents, with financial information required from both parents. The FAFSA focuses on the relationship of the student to the parents more so than the relationship of the parents to each other.

If the student's legal parents are divorced or separated and not living together, only one parent is responsible for completing the FAFSA, even if the parents file a joint federal income tax return. This parent is often called the *custodial parent*, but it is not necessarily the parent who has legal custody of the student or who claims the student as a tax exemption. The custodial parent is the parent with whom the student lived the most during the 12 months preceding the date the FAFSA is filed.[18] If necessary, count the number of days (nights) the student spent with each parent.

Sometimes, this criterion will not be sufficient to specify which parent must complete the FAFSA. For example, the parents might have joint custody and there might be an even number of days due to a leap year, or the divorce might have occurred less than a year ago. In such a circumstance, the custodial parent is the parent who provided more financial support to the student during the 12 months preceding the date the FAFSA is filed. If that is not sufficient, the custodial parent is the parent who provided more financial support to the student during the most recent calendar year for which parental support was provided. If all else fails, the college financial aid administrator will decide which parent is responsible for completing the FAFSA. Usually, the financial aid administrator will choose the parent with the higher income.

Parents who have a legal separation agreement can live together. Parents who have an informal separation cannot live together and should maintain separate residences. Different floors of the same postal address do not count as maintaining separate residences. Living in a hotel room on a temporary basis does not count either.

College financial aid administrators are aware that some parents manipulate the student's living arrangements in order to maximize eligibility for need-based financial aid. A student will sometimes qualify for more need-based financial aid if the student's parents are divorced or separated and do not live together and the student lives with the parent who has the lower income.

Fraud on the FAFSA

College financial aid administrators are required to notify the Office of the Inspector General at the U.S. Department of Education if a student or parent has provided false or misleading information on the FAFSA. This includes forgery of the student or parent's signature and other forms of fraud.

The penalties for fraud include fines of up to $20,000 and up to five years of jail time, in addition to repaying the financial aid received by the student. If the fraud involves $200 or less, the fines are capped at $5,000 and the jail time at one year.

Fraud may be reported to 1-800-MIS-USED (1-800-647-8733) or oig.hotline@ed.gov. Complaints may also be submitted online at **www.oighotline.ed.gov/hotline/**.

College financial aid administrators have more experience with detecting fraud than parents have in gaming the system. For example, the college financial aid administrator will be suspicious if the custodial parent does not live in the same state or even school district as the student's high school. Likewise, if the parents claim to be living apart, but the father answers when the financial aid administrator calls the mother's residence (or vice versa). College financial aid administrators may ask for proof, such as a copy of the divorce decree, separation agreement, utility bills or apartment rental agreements. Few parents go so far as to ask the court to modify the custody agreement.

If the parent is widowed or single (that is, never married) and does not live with the other legal parent, the student should answer the questions about that parent, not the other parent.

Divorced parents may be concerned about whether the noncustodial parent will have access to their income and asset information on the FAFSA. A federal privacy law, the Family Education Rights and Privacy Act of 1974 (FERPA), protects the privacy of educational records. The FAFSA and other financial aid application forms are considered to be educational records. The regulations at 34 CFR 99.12(b)(1) specifically preclude releasing parent financial records to the student. In addition, colleges will generally release financial information only to the parent who provided that information. If a college receives a subpoena seeking access to the FAFSA, it will generally notify the custodial parent so that the custodial parent can seek to have the subpoena quashed.

Children of divorced parents are less likely to enroll in and graduate from college. Based on data from the 2000 follow-up to the 1988 National Education Longitudinal Study (NELS:88), 56.4% of 8th grade students in 1988 whose parents were divorced enrolled in college by 1994, compared with 68.6% of 8th grade students whose parents were married. By 2000, only 28.0% of the students with divorced parents had obtained a Bachelor's or more advanced degree, compared with 45.1% of the students whose parents were married. Even if the students enroll in college, students with divorced parents are less likely to graduate. Based on data from the 2009 follow-up to the 2003-2004 Beginning Postsecondary Students longitudinal study (BPS:04/09), of students who enrolled in college for the first time in 2003-2004, 31.8% of students whose parents were divorced obtained a Bachelor's degree by 2009, compared with 45.1% of students whose parents were married.

Stepparents

If a widowed parent or the custodial parent is remarried[19] as of the date the FAFSA is submitted, the student should answer the parental information questions about that parent **and** the person to whom the parent is married (the student's stepparent). This can have a big impact on eligibility for need-based student financial aid.

A stepparent is treated like a biological or adoptive parent if the stepparent is married, as of the FAFSA submission date, to the custodial parent (the parent's whose information must be reported on the FAFSA). The stepparent's financial information must be reported on the FAFSA, without exception. Prenuptial agreements have no impact on this requirement, which is a matter of federal law.[20] The stepparent's income in 2014 must be reported even if the stepparent and custodial parent did not get married until 2015 (but prior to the date the FAFSA is submitted).

The stepparent's income and assets must be reported even if the stepparent refuses to help the student pay for college. There are no exceptions. Providing income and asset information on the FAFSA does not obligate the parents to borrow or cosign a student's loans or to pay for the student's college education. Parents are not responsible for repaying their child's federal student loans (e.g., Federal Stafford Loan and Federal Perkins Loan) even if the child is a minor. Federal student loans have not been subject to the defense of infancy since 1986. (The defense of infancy argues that a minor child lacks the capacity to enter into legally enforceable contracts. Federal law currently exempts federal student loans from the defense of infancy.) The child's federal student loans are also not reported on the parent's credit history. (The Federal Parent PLUS Loan, however, is reported on the parent's credit history, as are any private student loans borrowed or cosigned by the parent.) But, if the parents do not complete the FAFSA, the student will not be able to get any need-based federal student aid.

If the custodial parent dies, the stepparent is no longer responsible for completing the FAFSA unless the stepparent has legally adopted the student, even if the student continues to live with the stepparent. Instead, the noncustodial parent becomes responsible for completing the FAFSA.

If the student has not had any support or meaningful contact from the noncustodial parent for an extended period of time, the student can seek a dependency override from the college's financial aid administrator. In any event, support provided by the stepparent to the student should be reported as untaxed income to the student on the student's FAFSA in the answer to the question about "Money received, or paid on your behalf (e.g., bills), not reported elsewhere on this form."

Who is Not Considered a Parent?

Foster parents, legal guardians, grandparents or other relatives – such as aunts, uncles, or older siblings – are **not** considered to be parents for purposes of filing a FAFSA even if the student is living with them. The only exception is when this person has legally adopted the student.

Again, students should **not** provide any income and asset information about

- Foster parent(s) or legal guardians, because a foster child or a child who has a legal guardian is automatically considered an independent student.

- Grandparents or other relatives, because relatives are not considered parents unless they have legally adopted the student.

Students living with grandparents or other relatives must attempt to get parent information from their biological or adoptive parents. College financial aid administrators may consider using a dependency override to make the student independent in rare cases.

Any support provided by a legal guardian, grandparent or other relatives should be reported on the FAFSA as untaxed income to the student. Foster care payments are generally not reported as income on the FAFSA.

Parents' Marital Status

Report the marital status of the student's parents as of today. This refers to the marital status of the parents who are required to complete the FAFSA. Possible statuses include:

- Married or remarried

- Never married

- Divorced or separated

- Widowed

- Unmarried and both parents live together

There is a lot of potential for confusion in this question concerning the difference between "unmarried and both parents live together" and "divorced or separated" or "never married."

Parents' Marital Status	Parents Live Together	Parents Do Not Live Together
Divorced	Unmarried and both parents live together	Divorced or separated
Legal Separation	Unmarried and both parents live together	Divorced or separated
Informal Separation	Married or remarried	Divorced or separated
Never Married (Single)	Unmarried and both parents live together	Never married
Married or remarried	Married or remarried	Married or remarried

Note that if the student's parents are divorced and the custodial parent has remarried, the parents' marital status on the FAFSA should be reported as "Married or remarried." Likewise, if the student's parent is widowed and has remarried, the parents' marital status on the FAFSA should be reported as "Married or remarried."

If the student's parents indicate that they are married or remarried, they will be asked for the date they were married. Likewise, if the student's parents indicate that they are divorced, separated or widowed, they will be asked for the date of that status. The date should be of the most recent marital status. Recent changes in marital status may be subjected to greater scrutiny, especially recent informal separations, due to the possibility of a sham separation designed to increase eligibility for need-based financial aid.

Parent Information

Due to changes in the treatment of same-sex parents, the FAFSA now refers to the student's parents as Parent 1 (father/mother/stepparent) and Parent 2 (father/mother/stepparent) instead of father/stepfather and mother/stepmother.

For each parent whose financial information is reported on the FAFSA, the FAFSA requires the following information:

- Social Security Number

- Last name and first initial

- Date of birth

This information will be used with the IRS Data Retrieval Tool. Accordingly, the parent's name must match the legal name associated with the Social Security Number in Social Security Administration (SSA) records. Likewise, the date of birth must match.

The most common errors include use of a nickname instead of the legal first name, an error in the birth year and a failure to update the name in SSA records after a change in marital status.

Only the student must be a U.S. citizen, permanent resident or eligible noncitizen to qualify for federal student aid. The student may still qualify even if the student's parents are foreign citizens, undocumented or underdocumented.

If a parent does not have a Social Security Number, do not substitute a Taxpayer Identification Number (TIN) or stolen Social Security Number, as he or she will fail the data match with the Social Security Administration (SSA). Instead, enter 000-00-0000 as the Social Security Number. A parent who does not have a valid Social Security Number will not be able to use the IRS Data Retrieval Tool.

Parent Email Address

The parent email address is used by the U.S. Department of Education, the state and the colleges listed on the FAFSA to correspond with the parents, to confirm FAFSA data and to notify them when the FAFSA has been processed. The parent email address will also be used to remind the parents to update their financial information on the FAFSA if they indicated that they "will file" a federal income tax return as opposed to having already completed their income tax return.

The email address must be able to fit within the box shown on the application, with no more than 41 characters including the @. If the parent's email address does not fit, obtain a shorter email address from a free email service like Gmail.com or Outlook.com and configure it to forward the email to the parent's email address.

Parents may want to consider obtaining a separate email account to be used just for receiving information from the colleges and universities to which their children are applying. Some parents will configure this email address to forward all email to both parents, if the parents have separate email accounts.

It is important that this email address remains valid throughout the admission and financial aid application period.

Parent Household Size

The number of family members in the household is used to calculate a standard allowance for basic living expenses, the income protection allowance. This allowance, along with other allowances (e.g., federal, state and Social Security taxes, employment expenses, etc.), is subtracted from income to calculate available income. Increases in household size will reduce available income, resulting in greater eligibility for need-based financial aid.

The following persons should be included in the parent household size:

- The **student** applicant should always be counted in household size, even if the student is not currently living with the parents or is planning to attend college away from home.

- The **parents** should be counted in household size, except for parents who are not living in the household because of death, separation or divorce. Parents who are on active duty in the U.S. Armed Forces should be counted even if they are not living in the household because of the military service. If the student's parents are divorced, the custodial parent should be counted in household size. The noncustodial parent is not normally counted in household size. If the custodial parent (or a widowed parent) has remarried, the stepparent should be counted in household size, including any dependents of the stepparent.

- The **parents' other children** should be counted in household size, if the parents will provide more than half of their support from July 1, 2015 through June 30, 2016 *or* if the children would be considered dependent students (answering "No" to all of the questions in Section 3) if they were applying for financial aid. The other children do not need to be students or applying for financial aid to be counted in household size. Unborn children (including multiple unborn children) may be counted if they will receive more than half their support from birth through the end of the academic year. The parents' children are not required to live with the student's parents. Do not include siblings who are enrolled in U.S. military service academies, as the federal government covers their living and college costs.

- The **student's children** should be counted in household size, if the parents will provide more than half of their support from July 1, 2015 through June 30, 2016. Unborn children (including multiple unborn children) may be counted if they will receive more than half their support from birth through the end of the academic year. The student's children are not required to live with the student's parents.

- **Other people** (aunts, uncles, grandparents, noncustodial parents, etc.) should be counted in household size *only if* they currently live with the student's parents and will continue to do so from July 1, 2015 through June 30, 2016 *and* the student's parents provide more than one-half of their support and will continue to provide more than half of their support from July 1, 2015 through June 30, 2016.

Children of the student and children of the parents may be counted in household size even if they do not live with the parents because it is not uncommon for the parents to be supporting a child or grandchild who does not live with the parents. For example, the parents may be separated or divorced and the child might live with the other parent. The child will be counted in the household size if the parent provides more than half of the child's support.

Graduate and professional school students may be counted in the parents' household size on a sibling's FAFSA, even though they are automatically independent, if the parent provides more than half of their support. Note, however, that student aid funds received by a graduate or professional school student, including student loan funds, count as part of the graduate or professional school student's support. Often the support provided by the parents does not exceed the financial aid funds received by the student, in which case the parents do not provide more than half the graduate or professional school student's support.

When determining whether the parent supports a member of the household, it does not matter whether the parent claims the child as a tax exemption on the parent's federal income tax return. The support test used for federal student aid purposes is different from the support test used for federal income tax purposes.

Support is measured against the full year. If the parent starts supporting a child mid-year, the support provided for the remainder of the year must be more than half of the child's support for the entire year.

Support includes direct financial support, such as money, gifts and loans. It also includes food, clothing, housing, transportation (e.g., car payments, insurance, fuel and maintenance), medical and dental care and insurance, and college costs. It also includes indirect financial support, such as money paid to a third party to pay for expenses for which the child or grandchild or other person is responsible, such as cell phones, auto insurance and cable TV.

Whether the parents provide more than half support is measured by comparing support received directly or indirectly from the parents against support provided by other sources. The parents must count benefits received on behalf of the child as part of their support of the child. This includes money from government assistance programs (e.g., TANF, SNAP, Social Security benefit payments and child tax credits), not just the parent's income and assets.

Child Support and Household Size

If the parent provides more than half support for a child, count the child in household size and do not report any child support paid for that child.

If the parent provides less than half support for a child, do not count the child in household size, but do report the child support paid for the child.

Foster children are not counted in household size.

If a child is counted in household size, any child support paid by the parent for that child is not reported on the FAFSA. Only child support paid for children who are not counted in household size (i.e., children for whom the parent does not provide more than half support) is reported on the FAFSA. Child support paid reported on the FAFSA is subtracted from income by the FAFSA processor. If a person is counted in household size, an allowance for the support of that person is subtracted from income as part of the basic living expense allowance. Counting a child in household size and reporting the child support paid for that child would effectively double-count the support of that child. It is generally more financially beneficial to count the child in household size if the child is enrolled in college, since only children who are counted in household size may be counted in the number-in-college figure.

Number of College Students in the Parent Household

This question asks for the number of household members (excluding the parents) who will be enrolled on at least a half-time basis in a degree or certificate program at an eligible postsecondary institution during the 2015-2016 award year.

The number in college has a big impact on eligibility for need-based aid because the parent contribution portion of the expected family contribution is divided by the number in college. (The number in college is also used to reduce the income protection allowance because most living expenses for college students are considered separately as part of the college's cost of attendance figure.)

Only people who are included in the household size may be counted in the number-in-college figure.

The student is always counted in the number of college, even if the student will be enrolled less than half-time or is not residing in the parents' home.

Congress changed the rules to exclude the parents from the number in college in 1992 because this provision was prone to abuse. Parents with advanced degrees were enrolling in community colleges to increase their children's eligibility for need-based financial aid. In some cases, the parents didn't even pay the college bills for their sham education, allowing the registration to cancel for non-payment of the bursar's bill.

If a parent is genuinely pursuing a postsecondary education at the same time as his or her child, the parent should ask the college financial aid administrator for a "professional judgment review." Some colleges call it a special circumstances review or financial aid appeal. The college financial aid administrator will want to see proof that the parent is truly enrolled in college, such as copies of paid bursar bills and grade reports. Many financial aid administrators will verify enrollment with the other college. It helps to provide an explanation why the parent is enrolled in college, such as for job retraining or obtaining a more advanced degree related to the parent's occupation. Some financial aid administrators will increase the number in college to include a parent who is genuinely enrolled in college. Others will subtract the actual direct college costs (e.g., tuition and fees) actually paid by the family from parent income.

Students who are enrolled in a U.S. military academy are not counted in the number in college because the federal government pays for their college costs, not the family.

Students who are enrolled in an unaccredited institution that is not eligible for Title IV federal student aid are not counted in the number in college.

Parents' State of Residence

If the parents do not live in the United States, they should enter "FC" (foreign country) in response to this question.

Parent Financial Information

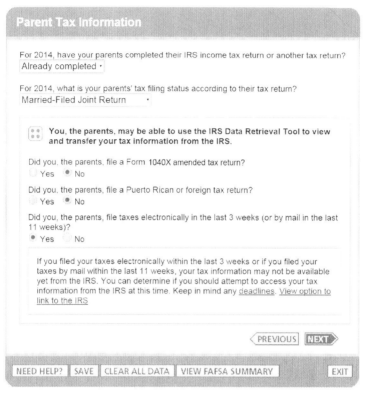

Once students have answered the demographic questions in Section 4, they will answer questions about their parents' financial information in Section 5. These questions are from the perspective of the parent. This section asks about 2014 taxable and untaxed income for the parent(s) as well as the current net worth of their assets.

Philosophy of Need Analysis

The student and his or her family have the primary responsibility for paying for college. The government and colleges provide financial aid when the family is *unable to pay*, not when the family is *unwilling to pay*. Student financial aid is not intended to subsidize lifestyle choices, so financial aid formulas will often distinguish between needs and wants.

Accordingly, most financial aid formulas, including the federal need-analysis methodology, are based on a philosophy that assesses a portion of discretionary income and assets.

- Discretionary income is the portion of total income that remains after allowances for mandatory expenses are subtracted. Total income includes taxable income (adjusted gross income) and untaxed income. Mandatory expenses include allowances for federal and state income taxes as well as a minimal allowance for basic living expenses.

- Discretionary assets are assets that are considered available to help pay for college costs. Certain types of assets are considered nondiscretionary, such as the family home, small family businesses and retirement plans.

Another aspect of need analysis involves basing the evaluation of a family's ability to pay on independently verifiable information. For example, the financial aid formulas usually split income into taxable and untaxed components because taxable income is verifiable by comparison with federal income tax returns and other documentation.

The financial aid formulas use a "snapshot" approach that measures income and assets at a fixed point in time, the date the FAFSA is submitted. Prior tax year income is not a perfect proxy for award year income, but the prior tax year is used as the *base year* for income because it is verifiable.

This yields a measurement of ability to pay that is independent of college costs, the expected family contribution (EFC). The EFC may then be compared with the college's cost of attendance (COA) to determine the family's demonstrated financial need. Demonstrated financial need is the amount of money the family needs in addition to their current resources to cover the college costs.

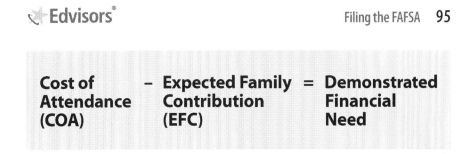

Cost of Attendance (COA)	–	Expected Family Contribution (EFC)	=	Demonstrated Financial Need

Financial aid formulas are also focused more on cash flow than on assets. Accordingly, the parent contribution portion of the expected family contribution (EFC) is divided by the number of children enrolled in college. Just because a family has two children in college doesn't mean the family can afford to pay twice as much.

Dependent student income and assets are assumed by the financial aid formula to be mainly available for paying for college.

Parents' Tax Return Filing Status

In this question, the parents are asked to provide information about their tax filing status for 2014:

- If the parents have completed a 2014 federal income tax return, the parents should select "Already completed"

- If they have not as yet filed their federal income tax returns, but plan to file a 2014 federal income tax return, they should select "Will file"

- If they have not and will not file a 2014 federal income tax return and are not required to do so, they should select "Not going to file"

If a student or parent selects "Will file" and supplies an email address on the FAFSA, the U.S. Department of Education will send a reminder to update the FAFSA after their federal income tax returns have been filed.

If a student or parent selects "Not going to file" but their income is above the filing threshold, their FAFSA will be selected for verification. Failure to file required federal income tax returns may affect the student's ability to receive federal student aid. Such a discrepancy represents conflicting information that must be resolved before the college financial aid administrator may disburse federal student aid. The income threshold for filing a federal income tax return is generally the sum of the standard deduction and the minimum number of exemptions that can be claimed by the taxpayer (e.g., one exemption for single filers and two exemptions for married filing jointly). The current income thresholds appear in Table 1-1 in Chapter 1 of IRS Publication 17.

(There is an exception to the timely filing requirements for active duty members of the U.S. Armed Forces serving in a combat zone. Also, taxpayers who file IRS Form 4868 to get an automatic 6-month extension must provide the college with a copy of their W-2 forms and must either use the IRS Data Retrieval Tool or provide a tax transcript after their federal income tax returns are filed.)

The parents are also asked about their tax filing status:

- Single

- Head of household

- Married – filed joint return

- Married – filed separate return

- Qualifying widow(er)

- Don't know

This information is used to identify discrepancies between the filing status on the federal income tax return and the marital status listed on the FAFSA. It may also be used to help select FAFSAs for verification. For example, the head of household status is error prone, since it offers a greater standard deduction than other tax filing statuses. Even if the federal processor does not select the FAFSA for verification, many college financial aid administrators will select the FAFSA for verification because of the likelihood of error involving the reported head-of-household status. Most taxpayers who claim head of household status do so incorrectly.

There are many criteria for head-of-household status, each of which must be fulfilled. According to pages 22-24 of IRS Publication 17, a taxpayer may file as head of household if all of the following are true:

- The taxpayer is unmarried or considered unmarried on the last day of the year.

  - To be considered unmarried, the taxpayer's spouse must not have lived in the home for the last 6 months of the tax year and the taxpayer must satisfy certain other criteria.

- The taxpayer paid more than half the cost of keeping up a home for the year.

- A qualifying person lived with the taxpayer in the home for more than half the year except for temporary absences, such as for school or military service.

The student's parents cannot both file as head of household if they live together in the same home. A student who is living with his or her parents cannot file as head of household, even if the student has a dependent child, because the parents, not the student, rent or own and maintain the home.

Tax filing status does not otherwise affect eligibility for federal student aid funds obtained through the FAFSA. It may, however, affect eligibility for certain education tax benefits. In particular, the American Opportunity Tax Credit, Lifetime Learning Tax Credit, tuition and fees deduction and student loan interest deduction are not available to taxpayers who file as married filing separately.

IRS Data Retrieval Tool

If the student's parents indicate that they have already completed their federal income tax returns, they will be asked additional questions to determine whether they can use the IRS Data Retrieval Tool. The IRS Data Retrieval Tool allows taxpayers to transfer information from their federal income tax returns to answer corresponding questions on FAFSA on the Web (FOTW). Millions of students and parents use the IRS Data Retrieval Tool each year.

Using the IRS Data Retrieval Tool may reduce the likelihood of the student's FAFSA being selected for verification. This will save the student and family time and hassle. Any data element that is transferred from a federal income tax return as filed with the Internal Revenue Service (IRS) *without modification* will not be subject to verification. Some colleges and universities require their students to use the IRS Data Retrieval Tool because it reduces the number of FAFSAs that must be verified by the school.

Who Can Use the IRS Data Retrieval Tool?

- Must have a valid Social Security Number
- Must have a FAFSA PIN
- Cannot file as married filing separately
- Cannot have a change in marital status after the end of the tax year
- Cannot have filed an amended federal income tax return (IRS Form 1040X)
- Cannot list a different home address on the FAFSA and federal income tax return
- Cannot file a foreign income tax return instead of or in addition to the U.S. federal income tax return

The IRS Data Retrieval Tool may be used to complete the initial FAFSA or to update the information on the FAFSA after the student and/or parent's federal income tax returns have been filed. Since many states and colleges have early financial aid deadlines, many families will submit the FAFSA with estimated income and tax information and later use the IRS Data

Retrieval Tool to update the information after their federal income tax returns have been filed.

Students and parents must use the IRS Data Retrieval Tool separately for their respective federal income tax returns.

The IRS Data Retrieval Tool typically becomes available the first Sunday in February and may be used 3 weeks after filing the federal income tax return electronically and 6-8 weeks after filing a paper federal income tax return. If a balance is owed on the federal income tax return, there may be a delay in the availability of the IRS Data Retrieval Tool.

To use the IRS Data Retrieval Tool, the taxpayer must have a valid Social Security Number and FSA PIN or FSA ID. Taxpayers who file a federal income tax return with a Tax ID Number (TIN) or use 000-00-0000 instead of a Social Security Number may not use the IRS Data Retrieval Tool.

Taxpayers who are married but file separate federal income tax returns (e.g., married filing separately or head of household) may not use the IRS Data Retrieval Tool. Likewise, the IRS Data Retrieval Tool will not be an option if the student's parents are unmarried but living together or if the student's parents have an informal separation but continue to file a joint federal income tax return (e.g., married filing jointly). Taxpayers who have experienced a change in marital status after the end of the tax year may not use the IRS Data Retrieval Tool.

Taxpayers who have filed an amended federal income tax return (IRS Form 1040X) may not use the IRS Data Retrieval Tool, since the tool can transfer data only from the original federal income tax return.

Taxpayers who have filed foreign income tax returns instead of or in addition to a U.S. federal income tax return may not use the IRS Data Retrieval Tool. This includes taxpayers from the Freely Associated States (the Republic of Palau (PW), the Republic of the Marshall Islands (MH), or the Federated States of Micronesia (FM)), whose Social Security Numbers begin with 666, as well as taxpayers who file a Puerto Rican tax return.

Taxpayers who list a different home address on their federal income tax returns than the home address listed on the FAFSA may not use the IRS Data Retrieval Tool. The two addresses must match for the IRS to confirm the taxpayer's identity.

Taxpayers who are victims of identity theft involving their federal income tax returns may not be able to use the IRS Data Retrievel Tool until the situation is resolved.

If a taxpayer does not use the IRS Data Retrieval Tool and the student's FAFSA is selected for verification, the taxpayer will be required to complete IRS Form 4506-T, Request for Transcript of Tax Return. Since it can take up to 30 days to process this form, it is best to request the tax transcript online or by calling 1-800-908-9946. It is no longer acceptable to provide the school with a photocopy of the income tax return, as some families were supplying colleges with a fake copy of the federal income tax returns.[21] The U.S. Department of Education now requires that the tax transcript come directly from the IRS to prevent this type of fraud.

If the applicant uses the IRS Data Retrieval Tool to update the student, spouse or parent information on the FAFSA, the applicant must submit the changes after using the IRS Data Retrieval Tool. Otherwise, the new data will not be transmitted to the college financial aid office. Submitting the changes is a final step that students and parents sometimes overlook.

Using the IRS Data Retrieval Tool is a multi-step process. First, the FAFSA will inform the parents that they are leaving the FAFSA web site.

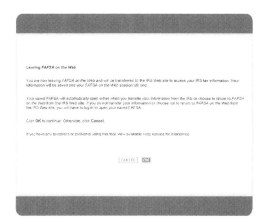

Next, a page will open on the IRS web site, asking the parent to prove his or her identity by providing his or her name, date of birth and some details from his or her federal income tax return.

Then, the IRS Data Retrieval Tool will display the information that will be transferred into the FAFSA. The parents can edit this information before it is transferred, but any information that is changed will not be marked as having been "Transferred from the IRS" and may be subject to verification. The transferred information will be used to pre-fill corresponding data fields on the FAFSA.

IRS.gov

Return to FAFSA | Log Out | Help

Español

Parent 2014 Federal Income Tax Information

The information below is your tax information that will help you answer some of the questions on the FAFSA.

	My Tax Information	FAFSA Question Numbers
Tax Year	2014	
Name(s)	Copper C Dog	
Social Security Number	***-**-8046	
Filing Status	Head of Household	
Type of Tax Return Filed	1040	Question 81 on the FAFSA
Adjusted Gross Income	$11,000	Question 85 on the FAFSA
Income Earned From Work	$10,000	Mother: Question 88 on the FAFSA or Father: Question 89 on the FAFSA
Income Tax	$2,200	Question 86 on the FAFSA
IRS Exemptions	1	Question 87 on the FAFSA
Education Credits	$0	Question 93a on the FAFSA
IRA Deductions and Payments	$0	Question 94b on the FAFSA
Tax-Exempt Interest Income	$200	Question 94d on the FAFSA
Untaxed IRA Distributions	$0	Question 94e on the FAFSA
Untaxed Pensions	$0	Question 94f on the FAFSA

Print this page for your records before choosing an option below.

Transfer My Tax Information into the FAFSA

☑ The tax information provided above will populate the answers to the appropriate FAFSA questions. After the FAFSA is populated your IRS session will end and you will return to your FAFSA. Check this box if you are choosing to transfer your information.

[Transfer Now]

Do Not Transfer My Tax Information and Return to the FAFSA

☐ By clicking the "Do Not Transfer" button, you are choosing not to transfer your tax information electronically. Your IRS session will end and you will return to your FAFSA. You may still use this tax information to input the data into your FAFSA.

[Do Not Transfer]

Foreign Income Tax Returns

If the parents file a foreign income tax return instead of a U.S. federal income tax return, they should complete the FAFSA using the corresponding figures from their foreign income tax return. For example, income taxes paid to a foreign government should be listed on the "U.S. income tax paid" line. Use the closest equivalent to adjusted gross income on the foreign income tax return.

All figures should be converted to U.S. dollars using the exchange rate in effect on the date the FAFSA is filed. Current exchange rates may be found on the Federal Reserve web site at www.federalreserve.gov.

Divide the foreign currency figure by the exchange rate to obtain U.S. dollars, and round the result to the nearest whole dollar.

The college financial aid administrator may ask for a copy of the foreign income tax return if the FAFSA is selected for verification. In some cases, the financial aid administrator may ask for a certified translation of the foreign income tax return.

If the parents file both a U.S. federal income tax return and a foreign income tax return, they should use the information from the U.S. federal income tax return to complete the FAFSA. The parents may be eligible to exclude some of their foreign income on the U.S. federal income tax returns by filing IRS Form 2555 or 2555EZ. The foreign income exclusion (line 45 of IRS Form 2555 and line 18 of IRS Form 2555EZ) should not be reported as untaxed income on the FAFSA.

> **Parent Financial Information**
>
> What type of income tax return did your parents file for 2014?
> IRS 1040
>
> What was your parents' adjusted gross income for 2014? This amount is found on IRS
> Form 1040-line 37.
> $ 21,000 .00   INCOME ESTIMATOR
>
> How much did your Parent 1 (father/mother/stepparent) earn from working (wages,
> salaries, tips, etc.) in 2014? This amount is your Parent 1
> (father's/mother's/stepparent's) portion of IRS Form 1040-lines 7+12+18.
> $ 11,000 .00
>
> How much did your Parent 2 (father/mother/stepparent) earn from working (wages,
> salaries, tips, etc.) in 2014? This amount is your Parent 2
> (father's/mother's/stepparent's) portion of IRS Form 1040-lines 7+12+18.
> $ 10,000 .00
>
> As of today, is either of your parents a dislocated worker?
> No
>
> In 2013 or 2014, did your parents receive benefits from any of the federal benefits
> programs listed below? Check all that apply or check **None of the above**
>
> ☐ Supplemental Security Income (SSI)
>
> ☐ Supplemental Nutrition Assistance Program (SNAP)
>
> ☐ Free or Reduced Price Lunch
>
> ☐ Temporary Assistance for Needy Families (TANF)
>
> ☐ Special Supplemental Nutrition Program for Women, Infants, and Children (WIC)
>
> ☑ None of the above
>
> You indicated that your parents filed an IRS 1040. Were they eligible to file a 1040A or
> 1040EZ?
> Select
>
> < PREVIOUS   NEXT >
>
> NEED HELP?   SAVE   CLEAR ALL DATA   VIEW FAFSA SUMMARY   EXIT

Parents' Adjusted Gross Income (AGI)

The next question asks about parents' 2014 adjusted gross income (AGI).
The AGI is the total of all income that will be listed on the 2014 federal
income tax return before it is reduced by deductions, exemptions and
tax credits. It includes earned income, such as wages, salaries, bonuses
and tips, as well unearned income, such as interest and dividend
income, capital gains, alimony received, business and rental property
income, unemployment benefits and the taxable portion of pensions, IRA
distributions and Social Security benefit payments. The AGI is reduced
by alimony paid, the penalty on early withdrawal of savings and certain
other above-the-line exclusions from income, such as the student loan
interest deduction, tuition and fees deduction, educator expenses and
moving expenses.

If the parents' AGI is $10 million or more, they should enter $9,999,999 as their income on the paper FAFSA.

If the parents have not yet completed their 2014 federal income tax returns, FAFSA on the Web (FOTW) provides an "Income Estimator" that can help them calculate an estimate of their 2014 AGI.

INCOME ESTIMATOR

Wages, salaries, tips, etc.
$ .00

Interest income
$ .00

Dividends
$ .00

Other taxable income (alimony received, business and farm income, capital gains, pensions, annuities, rents, unemployment compensation, Social Security, Railroad Retirement, and all other taxable income)
$ .00

IRS-allowable adjustments to income (payment to IRA and Keogh Plans, one-half of self employment tax, self-employed health insurance deduction, interest penalty on early withdrawal of savings, alimony paid, and student loan interest deduction)
$ .00

CALCULATE

Remember, if the custodial parents have not yet filed their 2014 federal tax return, it is ok to use estimated 2014 income information on FAFSA on the Web (FOTW). Estimates can be based on W-2 and 1099 statements, the last pay stub of the year from each employer, and the previous year's federal income tax returns. The parents will be required to update the FAFSA later, after they file their actual 2014 federal income tax returns.

In some cases, the student's parents will file a joint federal income tax return in 2014 but will experience a change in marital status after the end of the tax year but before filing the FAFSA. (It is also possible for a couple with an informal separation, as opposed to a legal separation, to continue to file federal income tax returns as married filing jointly.) If the student's custodial parent is now divorced, separated or widowed, only the custodial parent's portion of the income and taxes should be reported on the FAFSA. The parent's adjusted gross income (AGI) can

be calculated by adding the income from the parent's W-2 forms to other income extracted from the joint federal income tax return. For example, interest and dividend income from joint accounts should be split evenly, as should any adjustments to income that are attributable to the couple jointly, unless the couple has a legal agreement that specifies a different split. There are, then, two main ways of determining the taxes paid. The preferred method involves using the IRS Tax Table or Tax Rate Schedule for the separate AGI. The other method involves proportional distribution based on the percentage of the joint AGI that is attributable to the custodial parent. (Note that if the custodial parent has remarried, the new stepparent's income and taxes paid must also be reported.)

Income Earned from Work

These questions ask about custodial parent earnings from sources such as wages, salaries and tips. These questions must be answered whether or not the parents file a tax return. This information may appear on the parents' W-2 and 1099 forms, or on IRS Forms 1040, 1040A or 1040EZ.

The FAFSA instructions base income earned from work on

- The sum of lines 7 (wages, tips and other compensation), 12 (sole proprietorship business income and losses) and 18 (farm income) of IRS Form 1040 and box 14 (Code A) of IRS Schedule K-1 (Form 1065). If any of these items is negative, it should be treated as zero.

- Line 7 of IRS Form 1040A

- Line 1 of IRS Form 1040EZ

Combat pay should not be included in income earned from work.

Income earned from work is used to calculate an allowance for FICA taxes (Social Security and Medicare tax), an allowance for state and other taxes and the employment expense allowance. These and other allowances are subtracted from income when calculating the expected family contribution (EFC).

Income earned from work is also used instead of adjusted gross income (AGI) for people who are not required to file a federal income tax return.

Unfortunately, the FAFSA instructions do not correctly include all income earned from work. This usually leads to a higher expected family contribution (EFC), hurting the applicant's eligibility for student aid. The current instructions omit partnership income (which is usually reported on line 17 of IRS Form 1040), exclude retirement plan contributions (line 7 is based on Box 1 of the W-2 statements instead of Box 5), include taxable scholarships and fellowships (which are usually not subject to FICA taxes) and include the employer FICA contribution. The instructions also do not correctly address situations when the parents have two sole proprietorships, one with negative income that offsets positive income from the other. Nevertheless, applicants must follow the FAFSA instructions as written.

Dislocated Workers

The FAFSA asks whether Parent 1 and/or Parent 2 is a dislocated worker.

This question is prone to error, as many applicants misinterpret it as including anybody who has lost a job. It is important to read the definition of a dislocated worker carefully. If a parent is incorrectly reported as a dislocated worker, it may cause the FAFSA to skip some questions. When the FAFSA is corrected later, the applicant will need to answer those questions. This can cause delays in the receipt of financial aid funds.

A dislocated worker is defined in the Workforce Investment Act of 1998 (29 USC 2801) as a person who falls into one of the following categories:

- Someone who is eligible for or receiving unemployment benefits (or who has exhausted eligibility for unemployment benefits or was ineligible because of insufficient earnings or because the type of services performed weren't covered by the state's unemployment compensation law) because he or she was laid off or lost a job (or has received a layoff or termination notice) and is unlikely to return to a previous occupation.

- Someone who is terminated or laid off from employment (or received a termination or layoff notice) because of a permanent closure of, or substantial layoff at, a plant, facility or enterprise.

- Someone who is the spouse of an active duty member of the U.S. Armed Forces and either is a displaced homemaker or has lost his or her employment because of relocating due to a permanent change of duty station.

- Someone who is employed at a facility where the employer has announced that the facility will close within 180 days.

- Someone who is self-employed who is unemployed because of a natural disaster or because of the general economic conditions in his community.

- Someone who is a displaced homemaker.

A displaced homemaker is someone who satisfies all of the following criteria:

- He or she provided unpaid services to family members in the home, such as a stay-at-home parent.

- He or she was supported by income from another family member but is no longer supported by that income.

- He or she is unemployed or underemployed[22] and is having difficulty obtaining or upgrading employment.

Someone who voluntarily quits his or her job is not considered to be a dislocated worker.

Parent Financial Information continued

Enter the amount of your parents' income tax for 2014. This amount is found on IRS Form 1040-line 55.
$ 2,200 00

Enter your parents' exemptions for 2014. This amount is found on IRS Form 1040-line 6d.
1

Did your parents have any of the following items in 2014? Check all that apply and provide amounts.

Additional Financial Information

☑ American Opportunity Tax Credit or Lifetime Learning Tax Credit

Education credits (American Opportunity Tax Credit or Lifetime Learning Tax Credit) from IRS Form 1040-line 49
$ 0 .00

☐ Child support paid

☐ Taxable earnings from Work-study, Assistantships or Fellowships

☐ Grant and scholarship aid reported to the IRS

☐ Combat pay or special combat pay

☐ Cooperative education program earnings

Parents' Federal Income Taxes

This question asks for the amount of the parents' federal income tax for 2014. This question is based on the total income tax before the addition of other taxes, such as self-employment tax and household employment taxes.

The FAFSA instructions specify that the taxpayer should report line **56** of IRS Form 1040, line **37** of IRS Form 1040A or line **10** of IRS Form 1040EZ. This is the last line of the Tax and Credits section of the federal income tax return. It reports the total federal income tax, not the total taxes. It does not include any of the taxes listed in the Other Taxes section of the federal income tax return or "Health care: individual responsibility."

Self-employed individuals often wonder why the FAFSA doesn't include the self-employment tax reported on line 57 of IRS Form 1040 as part of taxes paid. The FAFSA calculates the employee's share of FICA taxes based

on income earned from work. This calculation occurs behind the scenes.
The employer's share of FICA taxes is excluded from the employee's
wages except for self-employed individuals, where the employer's share
of FICA taxes is subtracted from adjusted gross income (AGI) by line 27
of IRS Form 1040. So, if an applicant were to include self-employment tax
from line 57 of IRS Form 1040 as part of the taxes paid figure, the applicant
would be double-counting the self-employment taxes.

Report the federal income tax figure based on the specific lines of the
federal income tax return. Do not use a different line of the federal income
tax return or add other tax liabilities to this figure.

Other common errors include:

- Reporting the total tax line from the federal income tax return
  instead of the total income tax line

- Reporting the amount withheld by employers (or even one
  paycheck's worth of withholdings instead of the end-of-year total
  when using the last pay stub of the year to estimate)

- Reporting the amount of estimated tax paid

- Reporting the total payments from the income tax return or the
  amount overpaid

- Reporting adjusted gross income (AGI) instead of total income tax

Parents' Tax Exemptions

Report the total number of exemptions claimed on the parents' federal
income tax return, regardless of whether or not they are counted in
household size. Household size on the FAFSA and the number of
exemptions on the federal income tax return are based on different
definitions and are not necessarily equal. For example, exemptions are
based on the prior tax year while household size on the FAFSA is based

on the upcoming award year. The IRS and FAFSA also use different definitions of support.

The number of exemptions appears on line 6d of IRS Forms 1040 and 1040A.

IRS Form 1040EZ reports a combination of the exemption amount and standard deduction on line 5 instead of a number of exemptions. If the taxpayer does not check either of the boxes on line 5, report one exemption if the taxpayer is single or never married and two exemptions if the taxpayer is married. If either box is checked, divide line F of the 1040EZ Worksheet for line 5 by $3,900, the exemption amount per exemption.

Although the number of exemptions may differ from household size, college financial aid administrators may question a significant discrepancy between the two numbers. If this occurs, be prepared to explain this apparent discrepancy.

Additional Financial Information

Certain types of income and expenses are excluded from income by the federal financial aid formula. For example, the taxable portion of need-based student aid is excluded from income for federal student aid purposes. These exclusions are reported in the Additional Financial Information section of the FAFSA so that they can be subtracted from adjusted gross income when calculating the student's eligibility for need-based financial aid.

The exclusions from income include the following:

- Taxable earnings from need-based student employment, such as Federal Work-Study, teaching/research assistantships and cooperative education programs

- The taxable portion of scholarships, fellowships, tuition reimbursements/waivers and AmeriCorps benefits (education awards, living allowances and interest payments) that were included in adjusted gross income (AGI)

- Education tax credits, such as the American Opportunity Tax Credit and Lifetime Learning Tax Credit

- Child support **paid** (do not report for any children counted in household size)

- The taxable portion of combat pay

Families sometimes incorrectly report the full amount of a scholarship on the FAFSA. This question is intended to compensate for the portion of a scholarship or similar aid that was included in adjusted gross income. The taxable portion of scholarships and similar aid is typically written next to the line where wages are reported on the federal income tax return, along with the letters "SCH." The taxable portion of scholarships and similar aid reported on the FAFSA must match this figure. Do not report the tax-free portion of a scholarship or similar aid on the FAFSA.

Combat pay for enlisted persons and warrant officers is entirely tax-free. Only commissioned officers may have some taxable combat pay, generally equal to the amount that exceeds the highest pay for an enlisted person. Total combat pay is listed on the servicemember's leave and earnings statement. The untaxed portion is reported with a Q code in box 12 of the W-2 statement. The difference is the taxable portion of combat pay.

Some families may get confused by the child support questions. There are two questions, one for child support *paid* and one for child support *received*. Do not incorrectly report child support received in the child support paid question or vice versa. Report only child support paid

or received because of a legal requirement, such as a child support agreement, divorce decree or legal separation. Child support received outside of a legal agreement should be reported as untaxed income.

Federal Means-Tested Benefits Received by Members of the Household in the Last Two Years

This question asks whether anyone counted in household size on the FAFSA received certain federal means-tested benefits during *either* of the two previous calendar years (2013 or 2014).

The benefits include:

- Supplemental Security Income (SSI)

- Supplemental Nutrition Assistance Program (SNAP), previously known as food stamps

- Free and Reduced Price School Lunch

- Temporary Assistance for Needy Families (TANF)

- Special Supplemental Nutrition Program for Women, Infants and Children (WIC)

Check all that apply. Note that these federal benefit programs, especially SNAP and TANF, might have different names depending on the state. FAFSA on the Web (FOTW) might ask the applicant to report the annual benefit amounts received for each selected benefit program. Note that Supplemental Security Income (SSI) is not the same as Social Security Disability Insurance (SSDI), even though the acronyms are similar.

If anyone in the household received these benefits, it may make the applicant eligible for one of two simplified financial aid formulas, depending on income. The intention is to make it easier for the applicant to qualify for financial aid by providing additional methods of qualifying for the simplified financial aid formulas. Before these questions were added to the 2007-08 FAFSA, applicants and/or their parents had to have been eligible to file a particular type of federal income tax return (IRS Form 1040A or 1040EZ) to qualify for the simplified financial aid formulas.

Some families misinterpret the purpose of this question. It does **not** limit eligibility for federal student aid to just the families who received one or more of these means-tested federal benefit programs. In fact, about two-thirds of Federal Pell Grant recipients in 2007-08 did not check any of these boxes. It, likewise, does not reduce eligibility for student aid, nor does it reduce the household member's eligibility for these federal benefit programs.

Note that Supplemental Security Income (SSI) is not reported as untaxed income on the FAFSA, even though it can help the student qualify for one of the simplified financial aid formulas.

Parents' Untaxed Income

Certain types of untaxed income are counted by the federal need-analysis formula despite not being included in adjusted gross income.

These types of untaxed income include:

- Pre-tax contributions made by the taxpayer to qualified retirement plans, including deductions for pension plans, 401(k) plans, 403(b) plans, SEP, SIMPLE and deductible contributions to tax-deferred IRAs and Keogh plans

- Tax-free contributions to a Health Savings Account (HSA)[23]

- Tax-exempt interest income (e.g., interest on municipal bonds)

- Child support **received**

- Untaxed portions of IRA, pension and annuity distributions, such as a tax-free return of contributions from a Roth IRA (do not count rollovers)

- Housing, food and other living allowances paid to members of the military, clergy and others (excluding on-base military housing or basic military housing allowances, such as BAH, but not the basic allowance for subsistence, BAS). Students who receive free room and board, such as from a resident advisor position, should report the value of that compensation in the answer to this question.

- Veterans noneducation benefits (Disability, Death Pension, DIC) and VA Educational Work-Study allowances

- Other untaxed income, such as disability and workers' compensation (but not SSI), untaxed portions of Railroad Retirement benefits, black lung benefits, refugee assistance

The latter catch-all category does not include several types of untaxed income and benefits, including:

- Types of untaxed income and benefits that are excluded by the statute,[24] such as any form of student financial aid (including employer-paid tuition assistance), child support paid, Supplemental Security Income (SSI), earned income tax credit, the additional child tax credit, welfare benefits[25] (such as TANF, SNAP and WIC), income earned from a cooperative education program, AmeriCorps living allowances, untaxed Social Security benefits, the foreign income exclusion,[26] the credit for federal tax on special fuels, veterans education benefits,[27] per capita payments to Native Americans (only amounts up to $2,000), dependent care assistance (up to $5,000) and combat pay.

- Types of untaxed income and benefits that are not specifically mentioned in the statute, such as the foster care benefits, adoption assistance payments, heating/fuel assistance (LIHEAP), rent subsidies for low-income housing and contributions to or payments from flexible spending arrangements (cafeteria plans).

Generally, foster care payments are not reported as income on the FAFSA. If the foster parents adopt a foster child, the extended foster care and adoption assistance payments they receive under the authority of Part A (TANF) and Part E (federal payments for extended foster care and adoption assistance for children under age 21) of Title IV of the Social Security Act are not reported as untaxed income on the FAFSA. Other payments, however, may need to be reported as untaxed income to the student, per Dear Colleague Letter GEN-13-18.

The intention is to include untaxed income of a discretionary nature in total income. Non-elective pension plan and retirement plan contributions are not counted in untaxed income. For example, contributions to certain state public employee retirement systems, such as the IPERS (Iowa), KPERS (Kansas) and OPERS (Ohio) retirement systems, are involuntary and so should not be reported as untaxed income on the FAFSA. Contributions to a 401(k), 403(b) or IRA, on the other hand, are voluntary and must be reported as untaxed income on the FAFSA. Likewise, contributions by federal employees to the Thrift Savings Plan (TSP) are voluntary and, therefore, represent untaxed income. Note that employer contributions to retirement plans, health benefits and pension plans are not counted in untaxed income.

Note that the student's untaxed income figure includes cash support, while the parents' untaxed income figure does not. Cash support includes money, gifts and loans, plus expenses paid by others on the student's behalf, such as food, clothing, housing, car payments or expenses, medical and dental care and college costs. A dependent student does not report cash support received from his

IRS Form W-2, Boxes 12a through 12d

Elective Contributions to Retirement Plans
Code D – 401(k)
Code E – 403(b)
Code F – 408(k)(6) SEP
Code G – 457(b)
Code H – 501(c)(18)(D) tax-exempt organization plan
Code S – 408(p) SIMPLE plan

or her parents, except that cash support received from a non-custodial parent is counted as untaxed income if it is not part of a legal child support agreement.

Examples:

- If a dependent student's parents are divorced, cash support from the custodial parent and the stepparent (if the custodial parent has remarried) is not reported as untaxed income to the student. If the custodial parent dies, the stepparent is no longer considered a parent for federal student aid purposes. Accordingly, any support from the stepparent will be counted as untaxed income to the student. (The stepparent will no longer be able to borrow from the Federal Parent PLUS loan program, since the stepparent can borrow from this loan program only when the stepparent is married to the student's biological or adoptive parents.)

- Similarly, suppose that a student is living with his or her grandparents and the grandparents have not adopted the student. Any support the student receives from his or her grandparents must be reported as untaxed income to the student on the student's FAFSA. This support must still be reported as untaxed income even if the student is an orphan or the grandparents are the student's legal guardians (in which case the student is an independent student).

- If the student is an independent student, any support received from the student's parents must be reported as untaxed income to the student on the student's FAFSA.

- If a dependent student's parents receive cash support from the grandparents, it is not reported as untaxed income to the parents on the student's FAFSA.

Note also that only the amount of untaxed income and benefits actually received should be reported. For example, if an ex-spouse is in arrears on his or her child support obligation, only the amount actually paid by the ex-spouse should be reported, not the amount that was due.

The child support figure should include all child support received for any children in the household, not just child support received for the student.

Do not include foster care payments or adoption assistance payments in the child support received figure.

Roth IRAs are somewhat ineffective vehicles for college savings. Although the owner of a Roth IRA may qualify for a tax-free return of contributions, such a distribution must, nevertheless, be reported as untaxed income on the FAFSA. Eligibility for need-based aid is reduced by as much as half of untaxed income. One could wait until after the FAFSA is filed for the senior year in college to use a tax-free return of contributions to pay down student loan debt, assuming that there is no subsequent year's FAFSA to be affected by the untaxed income. But, contributions to a Roth IRA have low annual limits that are also capped at income, so there may be a limited opportunity for a student to accumulate significant contributions to a Roth IRA.

Some colleges and universities may ask for information about some of the excluded types of untaxed income. They are requesting this information for awarding their own financial aid funds, not federal and state aid. Some college financial aid administrators are dismissive of "paper losses," such as depreciation and net operating loss carry-forwards, since these losses usually do not affect cash flow. While these types of losses may be perfectly legitimate for tax-filing purposes, some college financial aid administrators do not consider them relevant to evaluating the family's financial strength and demonstrated financial need.

Simplified Versions of the FAFSA

The parents are also asked to specify the type of federal income tax return they filed or will file. The answer to this question and to the questions about means-tested federal benefit programs are used to determine whether the student qualifies for a simplified version of the FAFSA.

There are two simplified versions of the FAFSA:

- **Simplified Needs Test.** This version disregards all asset information.

- **Auto-Zero EFC.** This version sets the applicant's expected family contribution (EFC) automatically to zero.

A dependent student qualifies for these simplified versions of the FAFSA if

- The student's parents satisfy income criteria. The parents' adjusted gross income (AGI) must be less than $50,000 to qualify for the simplified needs test and less than or equal to $24,000 to qualify for auto-zero EFC. If the parents are not tax filers, income earned from work is substituted for AGI.

AND

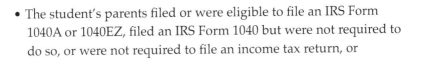

- The student's parents filed or were eligible to file an IRS Form 1040A or 1040EZ, filed an IRS Form 1040 but were not required to do so, or were not required to file an income tax return, or

- The student's parent is a dislocated worker, or

- Anyone counted in household size on the FAFSA received certain federal means-tested benefits during either of the two previous calendar years. These benefits include Supplemental Security Income (SSI), Supplemental Nutrition Assistance Program (SNAP), Free and Reduced Price School Lunch, Temporary Assistance for Needy Families (TANF) and the Special Supplemental Nutrition Program for Women, Infants and Children (WIC).

Similar criteria apply to independent students and the student's spouse (if any) for determining eligibility for the simplified needs test and auto-zero EFC, with one exception: Independent students without dependents other than a spouse are not eligible for auto-zero EFC.

Note that a dependent student's eligibility for the simplified needs test and auto-zero EFC depends only on the parent's income, not the student's income. It doesn't matter how much money the student earns; if the parent's income falls below the income thresholds and the parent satisfies the type of return test (or the parent is a dislocated worker or a household member received certain means-tested federal benefits), the student will qualify for one of the simplified versions of the FAFSA. This is in contrast with independent students, where the student's income does matter.

Iraq and Afghanistan Service Grant

If a student's parent or legal guardian died while serving on active duty in the U.S. Armed Forces in Iraq or Afghanistan after September 11, 2001, the student may be eligible for special treatment of his or her EFC if the student was less than 24 years old or enrolled in college when his or her parent or legal guardian died. If the student is eligible for a Federal Pell Grant, the student's EFC will be set to zero, qualifying the student for a maximum Federal Pell Grant. If the student is not eligible for a Federal Pell Grant because the student's EFC is too high, the student will receive an Iraq and Afghanistan Service Grant equal to the maximum Federal Pell Grant amount.

State Restrictions on Simplified Versions of the FAFSA

Although the student may qualify for the simplified needs test or auto-zero EFC, whether the student will be able to skip the asset and other questions depends on the student's state of legal residence. The FAFSA is used to apply not just for federal student aid, but also for financial aid from the student's state. Fourteen states and the District of Columbia do not allow students who qualify for the simplified needs test or auto-zero EFC to skip the questions. These include Colorado, District of Columbia, Georgia, Hawaii, Illinois, Minnesota, New Jersey, New Mexico, Ohio, Oklahoma, South Carolina, Vermont, Washington, Wisconsin and Wyoming. The answers to these questions, however, will not affect the student's eligibility for federal student aid. A student who qualifies for auto-zero EFC will still have a zero EFC for federal student aid purposes even if the student's state does not allow the student to skip some of the FAFSA questions.

Eligible to File IRS Form 1040A or 1040EZ

Generally, taxpayers are eligible to file IRS Form 1040A or 1040EZ if they satisfy the following criteria:
- The taxpayer earns less than $100,000
- The taxpayer uses the standard deduction
- The taxpayer does not receive self-employment income from a business or farm
- The taxpayer does not receive alimony

If a taxpayer was required to file Schedule D to report capital gains, he or she is not eligible to file IRS Form 1040A or 1040EZ. Additional information may be found in IRS Tax Topic 352.

Note that some paid tax preparers routinely file IRS Form 1040 even for taxpayers who were eligible to file an IRS Form 1040A or 1040EZ. Accordingly, this question asks about the type of form the taxpayer was *eligible to file*, as opposed to the type of form *actually filed*.

A taxpayer who is not required to file IRS Form 1040 but did so solely to claim an education tax credit, such as the American Opportunity Tax Credit or the Lifetime Learning Tax Credit, is considered eligible for a simplified version of the FAFSA.

Someone who is not required to file a federal income tax return, but filed an IRS Form 1040 only to claim the earned income tax credit, is considered eligible for a simplified version of the FAFSA.

Taxpayers who file IRS Form 1040 in order to itemize deductions are treated as though they were required to file an IRS Form 1040 even if this is the only reason they filed an IRS Form 1040. They may not select IRS Form 1040A or 1040EZ as the type of tax form they were eligible to file.

A taxpayer who files a foreign income tax return is treated as having been required to file the equivalent of IRS Form 1040. A taxpayer who files an income tax return for American Samoa, Guam, Puerto Rico or the U.S. Virgin Islands, however, is treated as having filed or eligible to file an IRS Form 1040A or 1040EZ.

Other reasons why an IRS Form 1040 may be required include a non-zero figure in any of the following lines of IRS Form 1040:

Income
- Taxable refunds or credits of local or state taxes
- Alimony received
- Business income and losses
- Capital gain or loss (ignore if Schedule D is not required)
- Other gains or losses not reported as part of capital gains or losses (Form 4797)
- Rent, real estate, royalties, partnerships, S corporations or trusts (Schedule E)

- Farm income
- Other income, such as net operating loss carry-forwards
- Foreign income exclusion (IRS Form 2555 or 2555EZ)

Adjustments
- Archer MSA deduction (Form 8853)
- Certain business expenses (reservists, artists and government officials)
- Health Savings Account deduction
- Moving expenses
- Half of self-employment tax
- Self-employed health insurance deduction
- Self-employed SEP, SIMPLE and qualified plans
- Penalty on early withdrawal of savings
- Alimony paid
- Domestic Production Activities Deduction

Deductions
- Itemized Deductions (Schedule A)

Taxes and Credits
- Taxable income exceeds $100,000
- Alternative Minimum Tax (AMT)
- Foreign tax credit
- Other tax credits (Forms 8396, 8859, 3800, 8801, etc.)

Other Taxes
- Self-employment tax
- Social Security/Medicare tax on tips
- Tax on IRAs and other retirement plans
- Household employment taxes

Payments
- Excess Social Security and Railroad Retirement Tax Act (RRTA) tax withheld
- Amount paid with Form 4868 (extension request)

- Other payments from Form 2439 or Form 4136 or Form 8865

Parent Asset Information

The net worth of parent assets is reported on the FAFSA. The net worth of an asset is the current market value of the asset minus any debts secured by the asset. If the net worth of an asset is negative, it is reported as having zero value on the FAFSA.

Net Worth = Market Value – Secured Debt

The asset value is reported as of the date the FAFSA is filed. In practice, this should be the asset value from the most recent bank or brokerage account statement received prior to the date the FAFSA was filed. If the FAFSA is selected for verification, the college financial aid administrator may ask for a copy of the bank or brokerage account statement to document the asset's value as of the date the FAFSA was filed.

If the family is buying or selling some assets before the FAFSA is filed, it is best to do this soon enough that it will appear on a bank or brokerage account statement received before the date the FAFSA is filed. Otherwise, the family should print a copy of the online bank and brokerage account statements as of the date the FAFSA is submitted and keep that copy in case it is requested by the financial aid administrator.

Note that only debts secured by an asset may be used to offset the market value of the asset. A margin loan against a brokerage account will reduce the net worth of the brokerage account because the loan is secured by the assets held in the brokerage account. If a credit card is used to buy gold coins, the credit card debt does not offset the market value of the gold, as the credit card debt is not secured by the gold. If the parents use a home equity loan on their principal place of residence to buy a vacation home, the full market value of the vacation home must be reported as an asset. The mortgage does not reduce the net worth of the vacation home because it is secured by the primary home, not the vacation home. The mortgage does reduce the net worth of the primary home, but this yields no benefit to the family because the primary home is not reported as an asset on the FAFSA.

A pending foreclosure or short sale against an asset does not reduce the net worth of the asset until the foreclosing party takes possession of the asset. In most cases, the asset will have a negative net worth, which will be reported as zero on the FAFSA. But, if a foreclosure, short sale, forfeiture, bankruptcy or involuntary liquidation results in some income to the family (including implied income from the cancellation of debt), college financial aid administrators have the authority to exclude this amount from income on the FAFSA.

If there is a legal claim against an asset that establishes a liability against the asset, that liability may be used to reduce the net worth of the asset. The statutory definition of the term "net assets" subtracts any outstanding liabilities and indebtedness from the market value of the asset.[28] For example, if a parent receives a lump sum payment for Social Security Disability Insurance (SSDI) benefits, normally the SSDI payment must be reported as income and as an asset on the FAFSA. But many long-term disability insurance policies include clauses that reduce the insurance payouts by the amount of any SSDI payments. These clauses require the insured to pay the lump sum SSDI payment to the insurer. The contractual obligation establishes a liability that offsets the lump sum SSDI payment. Accordingly, the SSDI payment should not be reported as income or as an asset on the FAFSA since the money belongs to the insurer, not the parent.

If an asset is owned by more than one person, the student and/or parents should report only their share of the asset. Unless a legal agreement specifies a different division, ownership of the asset should be divided equally.

Reportable and Non-Reportable Assets

Assets include any property that is owned and which can be bought and sold (i.e., an asset has exchange value).

Examples of assets that are reported on the FAFSA include:

- Cash[29]

- Bank accounts, such as checking and savings accounts

- Certificates of Deposit (CDs)

- Brokerage accounts

- Stocks, bonds, mutual funds, money market accounts, stock options, restricted stock units (vested portion only), ETFs, hedge funds, REITs, private equity and other investments

- Commodities and precious metals

- Businesses and investment farms (including the value of land, buildings, machinery, equipment and inventory)

- Real estate

- Installment and land sale contracts (including mortgages held)

- Custodial accounts, including Uniform Gift to Minors Act (UGMA) and Uniform Transfer to Minors Act (UTMA) accounts (if owner, not custodian)

- Trust funds

- College savings plans, including 529 College Savings Plans, Prepaid Tuition Plans (value is the refund value of the plan) and Coverdell Education Savings Accounts

The following assets are not reported on the FAFSA:

- The family's principal place of residence (the family home)

- A family farm, if it is the family's principal place of residence *and* the student and/or parents materially participate in the farming operation

- Any small businesses owned and controlled by the family. Small business have less than 100 full-time or full-time equivalent employees. To be controlled by the family, the family must own more than 50 percent of the business. Note that family members are not limited to just those counted in household size on the FAFSA, but may include relatives by birth or marriage.

- Qualified retirement plans, such as 401(k) plans, 403(b) plans, pension plans, annuities, traditional IRAs, Roth IRAs, Keogh, profit sharing, SEP and SIMPLE plans

- Life insurance policies, including cash value and whole life insurance policies

- Personal possessions, such as clothing, furniture, a car, computer equipment and software, television and stereo equipment

- Property received by Native American students under the Per Capita Act, the Distribution of Judgment Funds Act, the Alaska Native Claims Settlement Act or the Maine Indian Claims Settlement Act

Note that while qualified retirement plans do not count as assets, distributions from a retirement plan (including tax-free distributions) do count as income to the beneficiary on the FAFSA. (The only exception is for amounts rolled over into another retirement plan in the same tax year.) Tax-free contributions to a retirement plan by the taxpayer (not the employer) also count as income. Note that retirement plan contributions from the employer, such as an employer match of 401(k) contributions, do

not count as income. Likewise, insurance settlements from a life insurance policy do count as income.

The distinction between the income and asset treatment of retirement plans can be confusing. Qualified retirement plans are not reported as an *asset* on the FAFSA, but contributions to a qualified retirement plan and distributions from a qualified retirement plan are usually reported as *income*.

If retirement money is not held in a qualified retirement plan, it must be reported as an asset on the FAFSA, even if the asset owner has already reached the normal retirement age. The intent to use the money to pay for retirement is irrelevant, since there are no legal restrictions on the use of the money.

If the parents sell their principal place of residence, the net proceeds of the sale must be reported as an asset even if the parents intend to use the money to buy a new home. The parents could appeal to the college's financial aid administrator for a professional judgment adjustment. But, the financial aid administrator is unlikely to make an adjustment based on the family's intended use for the money. Financial aid administrators are more likely to make an adjustment if the purchase of the new home is imminent, with a signed purchase and sale agreement and the money is kept in a separate escrow account. Financial aid administrators are also more likely to make an adjustment if the sale of the family's home was due to a natural disaster, relocation or foreclosure or if the funds came from an insurance settlement or reconstruction loan.

Similarly, if the family gets a home equity loan or cash-out refinance to remodel the family home, the money must be reported as an asset until it is spent on the renovations. During an appeal for a professional judgment adjustment, it is helpful to provide the financial aid administrator with documentation of restrictions on the use of the money, such as clauses in the promissory note that require the family to use the money to remodel the home.

Money must be reported as an asset even if it is withdrawn from a bank account and stuffed in a mattress.

While money in a life insurance policy may be sheltered as an asset on the FAFSA, the high sales commissions, high premiums, low return on investment, the non-deductible nature of the premiums and the surrender charges, among other problems, may cost the family more than they save from sheltering the money from the need-analysis process. Distributions may also be reported as untaxed income to the beneficiary, hurting aid eligibility. Borrowing from a life insurance policy may lead to interest capitalization, eroding the cash value of the life insurance policy.

Failure to report a reportable asset on the FAFSA is considered fraud. There are many ways a financial aid administrator may detect unreported assets. For example, if the asset values are low compared to the interest and dividend income reported on the federal income tax return or if the assets are inconsistent with family income, it will raise suspicions. If there is any doubt as to whether an asset should be reported on the FAFSA, ask the college's financial aid administrator.

Double-counting as Income and Asset

Sometimes families complain that income received during the year is double-counted, once as income and once as an asset. This is true. If the income is a one-time event that is not reflective of the family's ability to pay during the award year, such as an inheritance or life insurance settlement, the family can ask the college financial aid administrator for a professional judgment review. Some college financial aid administrators will make an adjustment to exclude such one-time events from income. However, the money will still be counted as an asset.

Other Real Estate

While the family's principal place of residence is excluded as an asset on the FAFSA, the net worth of other real estate must be reported on the FAFSA. The net worth should be based on the current market value of the real estate minus any debts secured by the real estate. Given the recent volatility in the real estate market, the market value should be as up-to-date as possible.

There are several approaches to determining the current market value of real estate before subtracting the mortgage debt.

The best approach is to obtain a current appraisal of the property from a licensed appraiser. A real appraisal will cost a few hundred dollars and will be based on comparable sales. A similar approach is used by web sites like Zillow.com.

One could also use the most recent assessment for the real estate, if assessments are based on up-to-date market valuations. Unfortunately, many counties use assessments that are not based on current market values. Often, the assessments are out-of-date and may be unrelated to the current market value. Assessments are used to determine property tax, not to determine a reasonable market value.

Another approach is to use House Price Index data from the Federal Housing Finance Agency (FHFA) to derive a value for the residential property based on the purchase price and the year the property was purchased. This table is based on the national All-Transaction Index. To use this table, multiply the purchase price by the multiplier for the year of purchase. This will yield an estimate of the value of the property in Q4 of 2013.

Year	Multiplier	Year	Multiplier	Year	Multiplier	Year	Multiplier
1975	5.32	1985	2.56	1995	1.74	2005	0.92
1976	4.91	1986	2.39	1996	1.70	2006	0.88
1977	4.29	1987	2.26	1997	1.63	2007	0.89
1978	3.79	1988	2.14	1998	1.55	2008	0.95
1979	3.37	1989	2.03	1999	1.48	2009	1.01
1980	3.16	1990	2.01	2000	1.38	2010	1.02
1981	3.03	1991	1.94	2001	1.29	2011	1.06
1982	2.95	1992	1.90	2002	1.21	2012	1.05
1983	2.83	1993	1.85	2003	1.13	2013	1.00
1984	2.70	1994	1.82	2004	1.02		

Rental Properties

Rental properties are usually classified as investments, not businesses. This matters because business assets are treated less harshly by the federal need-analysis formula. Businesses may also be eligible for the small business exclusion, if they are owned and controlled by the family and have less than 100 full-time or full-time equivalent employees. To be considered a business, the real estate must be part of a formally recognized business and provide additional services (e.g., maid service). Renting out a vacation home, a time share or a room in the family's home is generally considered to be an investment. In contrast, a hotel is generally considered to be a business. College financial aid administrators may ask to see a copy of the property deed to determine whether title to the real estate is held by the business or the family.

Loans Held by the Parents or Student

Loans held by the applicant or the custodial parents (if the applicant is a dependent student) are considered to be assets. For example, if the student lends money to a friend, that loan is an asset since it will eventually be repaid. Likewise, a take-back mortgage where the seller of a house provides a mortgage to the buyer to help the buyer finance the purchase is considered to be an asset. Generally, the value of a loan is the principal balance of the loan, plus any accrued but unpaid interest. (The interest received from the borrower is reported on Schedule B of IRS Form 1040.)

College Savings Plans

Savings Plan Owner	Treatment of Assets	Treatment of Qualified Distributions
Dependent Student	Parent Asset	Ignored
Parent of Dependent Student	Parent Asset	Ignored
Independent Student	Student Asset	Ignored
Grandparent, Aunt, Uncle, Non-custodial Parent, or Other Third Party	Ignored	Untaxed Income to the Beneficiary

The treatment[30] of a college savings plan, such as a 529 College Savings Plan, Prepaid Tuition Plan or Coverdell Education Savings Account, depends on who owns the plan:

- If a college savings plan is owned by a dependent student or the student's custodial parent, it is reported as a parent asset on the FAFSA. This includes parent-owned college savings plans where the beneficiary is a sibling, not just college savings plans where the student is the beneficiary. Any distributions from such a college savings plan are not reported as income to the beneficiary or account owner.

- If a college savings plan is owned by an independent student, it is reported as a student asset on the FAFSA. This includes student-owned college savings plans where the beneficiary is a child of the student, not just college savings plans where the student is the beneficiary. Any distributions from such a college savings plan are not reported as income to the beneficiary or account owner.

- If a college savings plan is owned by anybody else, including a non-custodial parent, grandparent, aunt or uncle, it is not reported as an asset on the FAFSA, but any distributions from such a college savings plan are reported as income to the beneficiary (the student).

In all cases, non-qualified distributions are included in the beneficiary's adjusted gross income.

Note that if a parent owns a college savings plan for the student's sibling, that college savings plan must be reported as a parent asset on the student's FAFSA. A custodial college savings plan owned by the student's sibling is not reported as an asset on the student's FAFSA.

Contrary to claims that a grandparent-owned college savings plan has no impact on eligibility for need-based aid, it can have a very harsh impact on aid eligibility, since distributions are treated as untaxed income to the beneficiary, reducing aid eligibility by as much as half of the distribution amount. This represents a more severe reduction in eligibility for need-based aid than a parent-owned college savings plan, which reduces aid eligibility by at most 5.64% of the asset value of the college savings plan. For example, a $10,000 distribution from a grandparent-owned college savings plan may reduce eligibility for need-based financial aid by $5,000, while $10,000 in a parent-owned college savings plan may reduce eligibility for need-based financial aid by at most $564.

There are, however, a few workarounds for college savings plans owned by a grandparent or anybody other than the student or the student's custodial parent.

- Change the account owner from the grandparent to the parent before taking a qualified distribution. (In the case of a college savings plan owned by the noncustodial parent, change the account owner to the custodial parent.) If the state does not permit a change in account owner, the college savings plan may be moved to a state that permits changes in the account owner. Generally, it is best to wait until after the FAFSA is filed to change the account owner, so that the college savings plan does not need to be reported as an asset on the FAFSA and that year's distributions also do not need to be reported on the subsequent year's FAFSA.

- Wait until after the FAFSA is filed for the student's senior year in college to take a qualified distribution, when there is no subsequent year's FAFSA to be affected by the distribution.

- Wait until after the FAFSA is filed for the senior year in college to take a non-qualified distribution, when there is no subsequent year's FAFSA to be affected by the distribution. A non-qualified distribution could be used to pay down student loan debt. The income tax and 10 percent tax penalty on the earnings portion of a non-qualified distribution are usually smaller than the potential loss of eligibility for need-based financial aid from treating a distribution as untaxed income to the student.

The last two options assume that the student will not be enrolling in graduate or professional school in the subsequent year. The distribution must be reported as untaxed income if the student files a FAFSA for graduate or professional school for the following award year.

Qualified tuition plans are reported as assets on the FAFSA based on who owns the asset. As noted above, if the student is independent and owns the 529 college savings plan, it is reported as a student asset and qualified distributions are ignored on the FAFSA. If the student is independent and does not own the 529 plan, it is not reported as an asset on the FAFSA, but any qualified distributions must be reported as untaxed income. This includes 529 plans owned by an independent student's parent, as well as plans owned by grandparents, aunts and uncles. (Non-qualified distributions are included in the adjusted gross income (AGI) of the beneficiary.)

Note that the CSS/Financial Aid PROFILE form counts any college savings plan that lists the student as a beneficiary as an asset. This includes 529 plans owned by grandparents, aunts, uncles, non-custodial parents and other third parties. The PROFILE also requires parents to list assets for siblings who are under age 19 and not yet enrolled in college.

Home Equity Loans

A home equity line of credit (HELOC) is not reported as an asset on the FAFSA unless the borrower draws down cash from the line of credit. If the cash remains unspent, the cash must be reported as an asset on the FAFSA. Since the HELOC is secured by the real estate, not the cash, it does not offset the value of the cash.

Likewise, the unspent proceeds from a home equity loan must also be reported as an asset on the FAFSA.

If the HELOC or home equity loan is secured by the family's principal place of residence, it does not reduce the assets reported on the FAFSA since the principal place of residence is a non-reportable asset. If the HELOC or home equity loan is secured by a vacation home or other investment real estate, it will reduce the net worth of the real estate reported on the FAFSA.

Custodial Accounts

Custodial accounts, such as Uniform Gift to Minors Act (UGMA) and Uniform Transfer to Minors Act (UTMA) accounts, are usually reported as assets of the account owner, not the custodian or trustee. The child is the account owner. The parent is the custodian or trustee until the child reaches the age of majority. Accordingly, a custodial account is usually reported as the asset of the student, not the parent. The main exception is qualified tuition programs, such as 529 College Savings Plans, where a custodial 529 plan owned by a dependent student is reported as a parent asset on the FAFSA.

A Totten Trust ("In Trust For") is not a custodial account. When an account is titled "[Parent] In Trust For [Child]", the account transfers to the Child upon the death of the Parent. Such an account is considered to be a parent asset because the parent remains the account owner and can change the beneficiary.

A joint account ("Parent and Child") is an asset of both the parent and child. Unless the account specifies otherwise, ownership of the asset is split evenly among the account owners. Each account owner should report his or her share of the asset on the FAFSA. For example, if an account is owned jointly by the parent and student, each reports half of the net worth of the account as an asset on the FAFSA.

Trust Funds

Trust funds are generally reported as assets, even if access to the principal is restricted. The only exception is for trust funds that are involuntarily restricted by court order. (Restrictions placed on the trust by the person who established the trust are considered to be voluntary, even if the restrictions appear to be involuntary from the perspective of the beneficiary. For example, a life estate must be reported as an asset on the FAFSA despite the restrictions on access to the property for the duration of the grantor's life. Revocable trusts, Crummey Trusts and

Section 2053(c) Minor's Trust are also examples of trust funds that must be reported as an asset on the FAFSA.)

Accordingly, most attempts to shelter an asset from need analysis by placing it in a trust will backfire. The trust will still be reported as an asset, but the restrictions on access to the trust will prevent the beneficiaries from liquidating it. The trust will then continue year after year, reducing eligibility for need-based aid each year. (Some states allow the trustee to distribute the trust fund's principal for the education and medical care of the beneficiary, even if the trust fund restricts access to the principal.)

If ownership of a trust is being contested in court, the trust is not reported as an asset until the case is resolved and the estate is settled. For example, a testamentary trust is not treated as an asset while the decedent's will is being contested in court.

If a trust has more than one beneficiary, the student and/or parents should report only their share of the asset. If the terms of the trust do not specify some other method of dividing ownership of the trust, ownership should be divided equally.

Some trusts allocate principal and interest separately. For example, a trust might grant the income from the trust to a beneficiary for the duration of his or her life, and grant the remaining principal balance to a charity. If the trust allocates principal and interest separately, the trustee should use a net present value calculation to determine the corresponding asset value. This calculation discounts each of the future stream of payments to its present value, yielding the amount a disinterested third party would pay for the right to receive the future payments. The net present value is usually less than the sum of all the future payments. Typical discount rates include inflation rates or a risk-free rate of return (e.g., the interest rates on U.S. Treasuries of comparable maturity). In effect, the net present value is the amount someone would have to invest now to receive the future payments from the trust. The sum of the net present value of the principal and interest payments should equal the current principal balance of the trust.

The value of a trust is equal to its net worth. Any debts and liens against the trust's assets are subtracted from the current value of the trust's assets.

Illiquid Assets

Similarly, illiquid assets must be reported as assets on the FAFSA, even if they can't be sold or used as security for a loan. Illiquid investments include investments that cannot be sold without a significant loss. Examples of illiquid investments include restricted stock, thinly-traded stocks (e.g., penny stocks, microcap stocks), hedge funds, antiques, collectibles, partnerships, real estate, corporate bonds, closed-end funds and stock options (especially futures and forward contracts) must be reported as assets on the FAFSA.

Impact of Reportable Assets on Eligibility for Need-Based Aid

A portion of parent assets are sheltered by the federal need-analysis formula, based on the age of the older parent. This is called the asset protection allowance (APA). The asset protection allowance is intended to be the present cost of an annuity, which would supplement at age 65 the average Social Security retirement benefit payments to a moderate family income (as determined by the Bureau of Labor Statistics). In practice, the formula has little connection to reality and is very sensitive to the current inflation rate. Accordingly, the asset protection allowance may fluctuate by thousands of dollars from one year to the next. Typically, the asset protection allowance is about $30,000 to $50,000 for parents of college-age children.

The simplified needs test, discussed earlier, may cause all assets on the FAFSA to be disregarded if the parent income (for a dependent student) or the student's income (for an independent student) is less than $50,000, subject to certain other criteria.

Any remaining parent assets are assessed on a bracketed scale, with a top bracket of 5.64 percent. This is in contrast with a dependent student's assets, which are assessed at a higher flat rate of 20 percent without any Asset Protection Allowance. Often, a family can increase the student's eligibility for need-based student aid by saving in the parent's name,

instead of the student's name. If the family saved money in a custodial account, such as a Uniform Gift to Minors Act (UGMA) or Uniform Transfer to Minors Act (UTMA) account, moving the money into a custodial 529 College Savings Plan will cause it to be reported as a parent asset on the FAFSA, if the student is a dependent student.

Section 5 – Student Financial Information

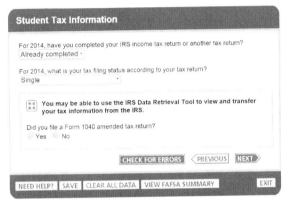

Section 5 also asks about the student's 2014 taxed and untaxed income as well as the current net worth of the student's assets. The treatment of student income and assets is similar to the treatment of parent income and assets, with an exception for cash support received by the student.

- Cash support received by a dependent student's parents is not reported as income on the FAFSA.

- Cash support received by a dependent student from the student's custodial parent(s) is not reported on the FAFSA.

- Cash support received by a dependent student from other sources, including the non-custodial parent, grandparents, aunts, uncles and other third parties, is reported as untaxed income to the student on the student's FAFSA.

- Cash support received by an independent student from all sources other than the student's spouse, if any, is reported as untaxed income to the student on the student's FAFSA.

If the student is married at the time FAFSA on the Web (FOTW) is submitted, the spouse's 2014 income and the current net worth of the spouse's assets must be reported in addition to the student's income and assets, even if the student was not married in 2014. Prenuptial agreements do not affect this federal requirement.

Independent students are eligible for the simplified needs test, but not all independent students are eligible for auto-zero EFC. Independent students with dependents other than a spouse are eligible for auto-zero EFC, but independent students without dependents other than a spouse are not eligible for auto-zero EFC.

Questions for Independent Students

There are some additional requirements that apply specifically to independent students.

Student Information (Independent Students)

This part of Section 5 asks information about those students who checked "Yes" to at least one of the questions in Section 3.

Student Household Size (Independent Students)

Your number of family members in 2015-2016 (household size)

> 1

The number of family members in the student's household is used to calculate the student's income protection allowance. The income protection allowance, which is based on a minimum standard of living, is subtracted from the student's income (and the spouse's income, if the student is married) to calculate available income. A greater household size will result in a lower figure for available income, yielding an increase in the student's eligibility for need-based financial aid.

The following persons should be included in the student's household size:

- The **student** applicant should always be counted in household size.

- The student's **spouse**, if the student is married, except if the spouse is not living in the household because of death, separation or divorce. A spouse who is on active duty in the U.S. Armed Forces should be counted even if he or she is not living in the household because of the military service.

- The **student's children** should be counted in household size, if the student (and his or her spouse, if married) will provide more than half of their support from July 1, 2015 through June 30, 2016. Unborn children (including multiple unborn children) may be counted if they will receive more than half their support from birth through the end of the academic year. The student's children are not required to live with the student.

- **Other people** (aunts, uncles, grandparents, elderly parents, etc.)
  should be counted in household size *only if* they currently live with
  the student and will continue to do so from July 1, 2015 through
  June 30, 2016 *and* the student (and his or her spouse, if married)
  will provide more than one-half of their support and will continue
  to provide more than half of their support from July 1, 2015
  through June 30, 2016.

Children of the student may be counted in household size even if they do
not live with their parents because it is not uncommon for the student to
be supporting a child who does not live with the student. For example,
the student may be separated or divorced and the child might live with
the other parent. The child will be counted in household size if the
student provides more than half of the child's support.

Stepchildren may also be counted in household size, if they pass the
support test, described below.

When determining whether the student supports a member of the
household, it does not matter whether the student claims the child as a
tax exemption on the student's federal income tax return. The support test
used for federal student aid purposes is different from the support test
used for federal income tax purposes.

Support is measured against the full award year. If the student starts
supporting a child mid-year, the support provided for the remainder of
the year must be more than half of the child's support for the entire year.

Support includes direct financial support, such as money, gifts and loans.
It also includes food, clothing, housing, transportation (e.g., car payments,
insurance, fuel and maintenance), medical and dental care and insurance,
and college costs. It also includes indirect financial support, such as
money paid to a third party to pay for expenses for which the child or
other person is responsible.

Whether the student provides more than half support is measured by comparing support received directly or indirectly from the student's parents against support provided by other sources. The student must count benefits received on behalf of the child as part of his or her support of the child. This includes

Child Support and Household Size

If the student provides more than half support for a child, count the child in household size and do not report any child support paid for that child.

If the student provides less than half support for a child, do not count the child in household size, but do report any child support paid for the child.

money from government assistance programs (e.g., TANF, SNAP) and the student's spouse or significant other, not just the student's income and assets.

Foster children are not counted in household size.

If a child is counted in household size, any child support paid by the student for that child is not reported on the FAFSA. Only child support paid for children who are not counted in household size (i.e., children for whom the student does not provide more than half support) is reported on the FAFSA. Child support paid reported on the FAFSA is subtracted from income. If a person is counted in household size, an allowance for the support of that person is subtracted from income as part of the basic living expense allowance. Counting a child in household size and reporting the child support paid for that child would effectively double-count the support of that child.

Number in College (Independent Students)

How many people in your household will be in college in 2015-2016?

1

This question asks the independent student about the number of family members who are or will be enrolled on at least a half-time basis in a degree or certificate program at an eligible postsecondary institution during the award year (July 1, 2015 and June 30, 2016).

The number in college has a big impact on eligibility for need-based aid because the expected family contribution for an independent student is divided by the number in college. (The number in college is also used to reduce the income protection allowance because most living expenses for college students are considered as part of the college's cost of attendance figure.)

Only people who are counted in household size may be counted in the number-in-college figure.

The student is always counted in the number of college, even if the student will be enrolled less than half-time.

Students who are enrolled in a U.S. military academy are not counted in the number in college because the federal government pays for their college costs, not the family.

Section 6 – Sign and Submit

Application Filing Tips

Before submitting the FAFSA, double-check the information for accuracy. In particular, be sure that the income estimates are as accurate as possible. Although the income information will be corrected later, after the family files its federal income tax returns, a significant difference in income or assets may cause a significant revision in the financial aid package.

- Every $10,000 difference in parent income may yield about a $3,000 difference in the expected family contribution (EFC) for middle- and high-income students, about half of that for low-income students.

- If the parents' income is close to the $50,000 threshold for the simplified needs test, even a small difference in income might cause a big change in the EFC if it causes the parents' income to cross the $50,000 threshold and the parents have significant assets.

- A $10,000 difference in student income may result in as much as a $5,000 difference in the EFC.

- A $10,000 difference in student assets can result in a $2,000 difference in the EFC, while a $10,000 difference in parent assets can result in a $564 difference in the EFC.

- Errors in household size can yield as much as a $1,700 difference in the EFC.

- Errors in the number in college can have a very big impact on the EFC, perhaps as much as doubling the EFC or cutting it in half.

Other application tips for filing the FAFSA include:

- Gather necessary documents ahead of time so that completing the application is faster and easier.

- Obtain the FAFSA on the Web (FOTW) worksheet from www.fafsa.ed.gov.

- Complete FAFSA on the Web (FOTW) by going to www.fafsa.ed.gov.

- Allow ample time to complete the FAFSA for submission by published deadline(s). File the FAFSA as soon as possible after January 1. Colleges and state grant programs may have their own deadline dates for applying for financial aid. Don't procrastinate. Some aid is awarded on a first-come, first-served basis. Don't wait until the day the application is due. Assume that the deadline is based on Eastern Time, not Pacific Time. (The federal deadline for filing the FAFSA is based on Central Time, but each state may use a deadline based on a different time zone for state grants. Assuming that the deadline is based on Eastern Time is safest.) Don't miss out on financial aid opportunities by missing the deadlines.

- Save work often. It can be very frustrating to lose one's work because of a computer crash or network glitch and to have to start from the beginning because the interim work wasn't saved. The password used to save the FAFSA should be different from the PINs used to sign the form. If the system indicates that the attempt to save the FAFSA failed, wait a minute and try again.

- The student and parents (if the student is a dependent student) should obtain PINs from www.pin.ed.gov to sign the application electronically.

- Students should keep a copy of all forms they submit and copies of all documentation used to complete those forms.

  ◦ Print and keep a copy of the FAFSA on the Web (FOTW) summary before submitting data electronically.

  ◦ Print and keep a copy of the Confirmation Page after filing the FAFSA.

  ◦ Print and keep a copy of the SAR after it arrives.

- Students should review the electronic SAR Acknowledgment or paper Student Aid Report (SAR). Make any necessary corrections using the student's FAFSA PIN.

- After students have been admitted to one or more colleges, they should watch for financial aid award notifications. These notifications are sometimes called financial aid awards or packages and will list the grant, scholarship, work-study and loan amounts the student might be eligible to receive.

- Remember, students must reapply for financial aid each year. Eligibility for financial aid may vary from one year to the next based on changes in the student's financial circumstances, changes in the number in college, changes in federal laws and regulations and annual updates to the need analysis formula's tables. Applying for financial aid by all published deadlines assures that the student is considered for the maximum amount of financial aid.

- Ask questions! Financial aid involves an alphabet soup of acronyms and technical jargon. It can be confusing. Students and their parents sometimes do not understand what to do next or what is required of them. Ask for help!

Need Help?

The U.S. Department of Education's Federal Student Aid Information Center (FSAIC) is available to answer questions from students and families about completing the FAFSA and federal student aid.

There are several ways to reach the FSAIC:

- Call 1-800-4-FED-AID (1-800-433-3243), toll-free, or 1-319-337-5665. (The TDD/TTY version for hearing impaired individuals is 1-800-730-8913.)

- Use the Live Help feature of FAFSA on the Web

- Visit the help section of the FAFSA on the Web at www.fafsa.ed.gov/help.htm.

- Send email to FederalStudentAidCustomerService@ed.gov

When calling the FSAIC to ask a complicated question about the FAFSA, write down the name and/or ID number of the person answering the question. This will allow college financial aid administrators to follow-up with the FSAIC if the answer appears to conflict with published

U.S. Department of Education policy guidance, federal regulations and federal laws.

Signature Page

If filing FAFSA on the Web (FOTW), it is best to sign the FAFSA electronically with a FSA PIN. (Starting in Spring 2015, the FSA PIN will be replaced with the FSA ID.) The student and custodial parent (if the student is a dependent student) must each sign the form separately with their own FSA PIN or FSA ID.

A FSA PIN may be obtained from www.pin.ed.gov. Students and parents should not share their PINs with anyone, not even each other. In particular, a dependent student's parents should not obtain a PIN on behalf of the student and use it to sign the form on the student's behalf, as that could be considered identity theft. By using a PIN, the person signing the form is certifying that he or she is the person identified by the PIN. The student and parent must each obtain their own individual PIN and read the certification statement before signing the form.

If the student or the student's parents are unable or unwilling to use a PIN to sign the form electronically, they will need to print and complete the signature page. There is an identification number on the signature page that allows the federal processor to match the signature page with the FAFSA. Mail the signed signature page to the address listed on the signature page. Submitting a paper signature page may delay FAFSA processing by several weeks, so it is best to submit FAFSA on the Web (FOTW) with a FSA PIN as early as possible. The signature page must be received by the federal processor within 14 days, or the FAFSA will be rejected. (If the student mails a paper FAFSA without the required signatures, it will be rejected upon receipt.)

When the FAFSA is rejected, the student will be sent a Student Aid Report (SAR) that indicates that the signatures are missing. If the student, the student's spouse (if the student is married) and/or the student's parent (if the student is a dependent student) sign the SAR and mail it to the federal processor, the reject flag will be cancelled and the FAFSA will be processed.

If a parent does not have a valid Social Security Number, the parent will not be able to obtain a PIN. The paper Signature Page represents the alternative way for this parent to sign the FAFSA. The student applicant, however, may still use his or her PIN to sign the form.

The FAFSA is a free form. You do not need to pay a fee to complete and submit the form. Some families, however, want help in completing the form. Free help is available from 1-800-4-FED-AID (1-800-433-3243) and College Goal Sunday (www.collegegoalsundayusa.org) as well as many high school guidance counselors and college financial aid administrators. If someone was paid a fee to provide you with personalized help or advice in completing the FAFSA, that person must sign the FAFSA in the paid preparer section and provide his or her Social Security Number or federal Employment Identification Number (EIN). People who provide free help in completing the FAFSA, such as high school guidance counselors and college financial aid administrators, are not considered paid preparers. If a paid preparer refuses to sign the form or fails to disclose that the form may be completed for free without professional assistance, be wary of any information provided by the preparer. The student and parents should not share their PINs with anyone.

If the student's parents are unable to sign the form because of a physical or mental impairment, because their current location is unknown or because they are "not currently in the United States and cannot be contacted by normal means," a high school guidance counselor or college financial aid administrator may sign the form instead of the parent. This is merely to get the form processed; the counselor or aid administrator does not assume any liability for the information provided on the form. The counselor or aid administrator should sign the signature page or the paper FAFSA, writing his or her title in parentheses after his or her name. The counselor or aid administrator should also write the reason why he or she is signing for the parents.

If the applicant submits a paper version of the FAFSA before January 1, the FAFSA will be processed, but will be rejected. The student and custodial parent (if the student is a dependent student) must sign the SAR to reaffirm the accuracy of the information on the FAFSA before the federal processor can finish processing the form.

Web Certification Statement

By signing the form, the student applicant, the student's parents and the paid preparer are certifying that all of the information on the form is accurate and that they are willing to provide documents during verification to prove that the information is correct. This information may include income tax returns (e.g., requesting a tax transcript from the IRS) and other documentation requested by the college financial aid administrator. The U.S. Department of Education has the authority to verify information reported on the FAFSA with the IRS, Social Security Administration, VA and other federal agencies.

The student also certifies the following:

- **Statement of Educational Purpose.** The student agrees to use federal and/or state student financial aid only to pay the cost of attending an institution of higher education.

- **Not in default.** The student certifies that he or she is not in default on a federal student loan or has made satisfactory arrangements to repay the loan.

- **Does not owe a grant refund.** The student certifies that he or she does not owe money back on a federal student grant or has made satisfactory arrangements to repay the grant overpayment.

- **Notify school about defaults.** The student agrees to notify his or her school if he or she defaults on a federal student loan.

- **No duplicate Federal Pell Grants.** The student agrees that he or she will not receive a Federal Pell Grant for attendance at more than one college or university for the same period of time.

Signing the form also gives permission for the U.S. Department of Education to release the data to the student's state of legal residence, the colleges listed on the form and the states in which those colleges are located.

Section 7 – Confirmation

After the student and custodial parent sign FAFSA on the Web (FOTW) with their PINs, FOTW will display a Confirmation Page. Print a copy of the Confirmation Page, as it represents proof that the FAFSA was filed prior to the student receiving the Student Aid Report (SAR).

In addition to confirming submission of FAFSA on the Web (FOTW) to the U.S. Department of Education, this page shows the student's Expected Family Contribution (EFC), Estimated Federal Pell Grant and Federal Stafford Loan eligibility, as well as the list of schools scheduled to receive FAFSA data.

The Confirmation Page may also be used to transfer the FAFSA information into a state's financial aid application form. Currently nine states allow such a transfer: California, Indiana, Iowa, Minnesota, Mississippi, New Jersey, New York, Pennsylvania and Vermont.

The Confirmation Page may also be used to transfer the parent's information into the FAFSA of the student's siblings, saving the parent some time.

Each time a student makes FAFSA on the Web corrections, a new Confirmation Page will be available which will reflect the changes made.

My FAFSA Page

The "My FAFSA" page may be used to make corrections to the FAFSA, view the Student Aid Report, view the correction history and provide missing signatures.

Step 4 – NEXT STEPS

What Happens Next?

Within two weeks after filing the FAFSA, the student should receive a Student Aid Report (SAR) from the federal processor. The SAR summarizes the information the family provided on the FAFSA. Each school listed on the SAR will also receive the information electronically. (The school's version of the SAR is called an Institutional Student Information Record (ISIR).)

Generally, students will receive a link to the SAR by email within 3-5 days if they filed the FAFSA online, signed it with PINs and provided a valid email address on the form. If the student did not provide a valid email address, a paper copy of the SAR will arrive within 7-10 days. If the student printed and mailed the signature page instead of signing the form with a PIN, a paper copy of the SAR will arrive within 2 weeks. If the student filed a paper FAFSA and provided a valid email address, a link to the SAR should arrive by email within 2 weeks. If the student did not provide a valid email address, a paper SAR should arrive within 3 weeks.

If a student does not receive the SAR within three weeks, he or she should contact the federal processor to check on the status of the FAFSA. Check on the status of the FAFSA by calling 1-800-4-FED AID (1-800-433-3243) or by visiting the FAFSA on the Web (FOTW) web site (use the PIN to login) at www.fafsa.ed.gov.

Once each school receives the electronic SAR and all other required financial aid forms, and confirms the student's admission status, the financial aid office will determine the student's financial aid eligibility. Some schools may request that the student submit income documentation such as student and parent 2014 federal income tax returns, including W-2s and all schedules and attachments, before sending the student a final determination of federal student aid eligibility. The school will use this and any other requested information to verify the accuracy of the data provided on the FAFSA. Schools understand that many families have used estimated data.

A financial aid notification (commonly referred to as a financial aid award letter) describing the amounts and sources of aid the student has been awarded will be prepared for the student when the student's financial aid application is complete. Most schools will wait until the student has been accepted for admission to notify him or her about financial aid eligibility, typically in late March or early April. The student then has until the National Candidates Reply Date of May 1 to accept the financial aid offer along with admission to the college. Returning students may receive their award letters a few months later. Some schools will mail a paper financial aid award to the student; others may provide the award electronically.

In some cases, the student will be required to sign and return a copy of the financial aid award notification, indicating whether he or she accepts or declines each source of aid.

If family circumstances change after the student completes the FAFSA and other required financial aid documents, students should make sure to contact the financial aid office at each school as soon as possible. See "Adjustments" section.

Comparing Award Letters

When comparing financial aid award letters from different colleges, calculate the net price of each award letter. The *net price* is the difference between the total cost of attendance and just the grants, scholarships and other gift aid. (Be careful to distinguish between loans and grants, as some financial aid award letters can be confusing. A loan does not reduce college costs.) The net price is the amount the student and his or her family will have to pay from savings, income and loans to cover the college costs. Think of it as a discounted sticker price.

There are, however, two caveats about the net price:

- **Front-loading of grants.** About half of all colleges practice front-loading of grants, which provides a better mix of grants to first-year students than to upperclassmen. This will yield a lower net price during the freshman year than during subsequent years. Ask the college whether it practices front-loading of grants, or visit College Navigator at http://nces.ed.gov/collegenavigator/ and use the financial aid section to compare the percentage receiving "Grant or scholarship aid" and the average grant or scholarship aid amount for *beginning* undergraduate students and *all* undergraduate students. If the college practices front-loading of grants, there will be a significant difference in these figures.

- **Scholarship displacement.** All colleges must adjust the need-based financial aid package when a student wins a private scholarship. But, each college can choose how to adjust the financial aid package. Some colleges will use the private scholarship to reduce or eliminate unmet financial need, if any. Then, some colleges will use the private scholarship to reduce loans and/or student employment, in which case the student's net price will decrease. Other colleges will use the private scholarship to reduce the college's own grant funds, in which case the student gets no net financial benefit. Students should ask each college for a copy of its "outside scholarship policy" if they've won private scholarships. It can make a big difference in the net price.

Some colleges have adopted the Financial Aid Shopping Sheet, which is a standardized one-page summary of the financial aid award letter, including a personalized net price. But, be careful, as some colleges will include a *net cost* figure on the shopping sheet in addition to the net price figure. The net cost subtracts the entire financial aid package, including loans and student employment, from the cost of attendance, making the college look less expensive than it really is.

Student Aid Report (SAR)

A SAR Acknowledgment will be sent electronically if the student provides an email address on the FAFSA on the Web. If the student does not provide an email address, a paper SAR will be mailed to the student at the student's permanent home address that was listed on the FAFSA.

The SAR includes the student's expected family contribution (EFC) and an estimate of the student's eligibility for the Federal Pell Grant. The SAR also includes information about each of the colleges listed on the FAFSA, including graduation rates, retention rates and transfer rates. The graduation rate is the percentage of students receiving a degree or certificate within 150% of the normal timeframe for attaining a degree or certificate (e.g., 6 years for a 4-year program). The retention rate is the percentage of first-time, first-year undergraduate students who return to the college the next year. The transfer rate is the percentage of the first-time, first-year undergraduate students who transfer to another college within 150% of the normal timeframe for attaining a degree or certificate.

The student can make corrections on the electronic or paper SAR.

Some data elements on the SAR will be marked with an asterisk. If the applicant left some fields blank, the federal processor may make reasonable assumptions about the values based on other information provided on the FAFSA. For example, if the student filed a federal income tax return but left the adjusted gross income (AGI) field blank, the federal processor will set the field to the value of the student's income earned from work (plus the income earned from work of the student's spouse, if the student is married). These fields should be corrected if the assumed values are incorrect.

The student can add additional colleges to the SAR or change the list of colleges on FAFSA on the Web (FOTW). These colleges will then be sent the student's information. Colleges can also obtain a student's SAR if the student provides the college financial aid administrator with the four-digit Data Release Number (DRN) from the upper right corner of the first page of the paper SAR. (On an electronic SAR, the DRN appears below the EFC in the box with the application receipt date.)

Each college or university the student lists in Section 2 on the FAFSA will receive an Institutional Student Information Report or "ISIR." This is an electronic record of all the information the student and his or her family reported on the FAFSA.

Students should keep a copy of the SAR with the rest of their financial aid documents. Private scholarship providers may also require a copy of the SAR as part of their application materials.

INCREASING ELIGIBILITY FOR NEED-BASED FINANCIAL AID

There are several strategies that a family can use to improve the student's eligibility for need-based financial aid by reducing the expected family contribution (EFC). Some of these strategies involve repositioning the family's income and assets. Other strategies involve tweaking the family's demographic information.

Tell the Truth

Do not lie on the FAFSA. There's a difference between using insights into the financial aid formula to avoid making mistakes that hurt the student's financial aid eligibility and lying about one's income, assets and demographic information.

People who lie on financial aid application forms are often caught. About one-third of FAFSAs are selected for verification, where the applicant has to provide copies of independent third-party documentation of the data reported on the FAFSA. In contrast, the Internal Revenue Service (IRS) audits only about one percent of federal income tax returns. Financial aid administrators have more experience detecting fraud on financial aid forms than families have in perpetrating fraud. Inconsistencies between information reported on the FAFSA and federal income tax returns often reveal unreported income and assets. The IRS and the U.S. Department of Education continue to share data to improve accuracy and detect fraud on the FAFSA. (The IRS does not, however, currently use FAFSA data to detect fraud on federal income tax returns.)

Intentionally providing false and misleading information on the FAFSA is fraud. The penalties for lying on the FAFSA include, but are not limited to, fines of up to $20,000 and up to five years of jail time, in addition to repaying the financial aid received by the student. Some colleges and universities will suspend or expel a student for providing false information on financial aid application forms.

Test Strategies First

Before using any strategy, test it by playing a what-if game with an EFC calculator. Don't waste time and effort on implementing a strategy that doesn't affect the student's EFC. For example, if the family qualifies for the simplified needs test, there is no point in shifting assets from the child's name to the parent's name, since all assets will be disregarded.

Optimizing Income

Avoid Artificial Increases in Income

The expected family contribution is heavily weighted toward income. A $10,000 change in income will have a much bigger impact on eligibility for need-based aid than a $10,000 change in assets. So, it is important to avoid artificially increasing the student and parent income during the prior year.

- Capital gains. Be careful about selling investments the year before the child applies for need-based financial aid. Capital gains are included in adjusted gross income and can affect eligibility for need-based financial aid. If the parents need to sell investments to pay for college costs, they should either do this at least two years before the child enrolls in college (e.g., before January 1 of the child's junior year in high school) or offset the capital gains with capital losses.

- Retirement plan distributions. Retirement plan distributions count as income on the FAFSA and should be avoided, if at all possible. There is no exception for hardship distributions, such as a distribution to buy or repair a home, prevent foreclosure or eviction, pay for medical expenses or pay for tuition. (The family could appeal to the college financial aid administrator for an adjustment to income corresponding to the hardship distribution, but there's no guarantee that the financial aid administrator will make the adjustment.) The financial benefit of taking a distribution is often small due to the combination of the tax impact and the financial aid impact.

- A tax-free return of contributions from a Roth IRA is reported as untaxed income on the FAFSA, which has the same impact on aid eligibility as increasing adjusted gross income. If the student or parents wish to take a tax-free return of contributions from a Roth IRA, they should wait until after the FAFSA is filed for the student's senior year in college. If the student will not be going to graduate or professional school, there will be no subsequent year's FAFSA to be affected by the distribution. The distribution can then be used to pay down student loan debt.

- If the family converts a traditional IRA into a Roth IRA, they should appeal to the college financial aid administrator to get the conversion disregarded as income, assuming that the full amount of the distribution was rolled over into the Roth IRA. The U.S. Department of Education issued guidance in Dear Colleague Letter GEN-99-10 to encourage college financial aid administrators to make such an adjustment.

- One-time events. Receiving a bonus or exercising stock options can increase income in a way that may not be reflective of the family's ability to pay for college. While some colleges may adjust the family income (but not assets) to exclude one-time events, some will not, especially if the event was within the family's control.

- Pass-through entities. Income received by a pass-through entity, such as a sole proprietorship, partnership, S corporation or LLC, is treated as income to the owner(s) even if the money is retained by the business to pay for future expenses. Small businesses owned and controlled by the family may be excluded as assets on the FAFSA, due to the small business exclusion, but the business income is still reported as income on the FAFSA. (The small business exclusion requires the business to be owned and controlled by the family and to have less than 100 full-time and full-time-equivalent employees.) Business owners may be able to offset this income by accelerating business expenses. Business owners could also change the form of the business to a non-pass-through entity, such as a C corporation. However, the higher tax on a C corporation's profits may offset the increased eligibility for need-based financial aid.

- Gifts. Gifts from grandparents or other relatives to the student must be reported as untaxed income on the student's FAFSA, hurting eligibility for need-based aid. Gifts to the student's parents, however, are not reported as untaxed income on the FAFSA, although the money is still reported as an asset. An alternative is to have the grandparents contribute to a 529 College Savings Plan owned by the student or parents. Grandparents could also wait until after the student graduates from college to help the student pay down his or her student loans as a graduation present.

Retirement Plan Loans

While a loan from a 401(k) retirement plan may avoid the impact on income of a distribution from a retirement plan, there are other problems with retirement plan loans. If the loan proceeds are obtained before the family files the FAFSA and are not spent until after the FAFSA is filed, the money must be reported as an asset on the FAFSA. A 401(k) loan must be repaid within five years or sooner, if the employee loses his or her job. Failure to repay the loan will result in the loan being treated as a distribution. The employee may be precluded from contributing to the retirement plan until the loan has been repaid, potentially causing the employee to miss the opportunity to receive matching contributions from the employer. The interest earned on the loan merely replaces the earnings the money would have earned had it remained invested in the 401(k). The interest paid on a 401(k) loan is not eligible for deductions. In contrast, up to $2,500 in interest paid on federal and private education loans is eligible for an above-the-line exclusion from income, which can be claimed even if the taxpayer does not itemize.

Threshold Effects

There are two important income thresholds that can have a big impact on the EFC. Families with income close to these thresholds may be able to increase eligibility for financial aid by reducing income slightly (or avoiding an artificial increase in income).

- Simplified Needs Test. If the adjusted gross income (AGI) of a dependent student's parents is less than $50,000 and the parents satisfy certain other criteria, one of which is the requirement that the parents were eligible to file IRS Form 1040A or 1040EZ, the simplified needs test will cause all assets to be disregarded. This same treatment is true for the income of an independent student and the student's spouse (if the student is married).

- Auto-zero EFC. If the adjusted gross income (AGI) of a dependent student's parents is less than or equal to $24,000 and the parents satisfy certain other criteria, one of which is the requirement that the parents were eligible to file IRS Form 1040A or 1040EZ, auto-zero EFC will cause the student's EFC to be automatically set to zero. This same approach applies for the income of an independent student and the student's spouse (if the student is married), if the student has dependents other than a spouse.

The parents may be able to reduce their income slightly by taking an unpaid leave of absence, offsetting up to $3,000 in income by realizing a capital loss, increasing retirement plan contributions, deferring income and bonuses into the next year, claiming the student loan interest deduction or claiming the tuition and fees deduction. Increasing retirement plan contributions does not reduce total income on the FAFSA, but it does reduce adjusted gross income (AGI), which may affect eligibility for the simplified needs test.

Using a capital loss to reduce income may not be effective for all parents. Realizing a capital loss may preclude the parents from qualifying for the simplified needs test and auto-zero EFC by filing IRS Form 1040A or 1040EZ.

Changes in Income vs. Changes in the EFC

Note that a reduction in income generally does not increase eligibility for need-based financial aid by more than the after-tax change in net income. So, aside from threshold effects caused by the simplified needs test and auto-zero EFC, it generally does not pay to work less to increase aid eligibility. Earning more money usually gives the family more

options. Still, there are other costs that the family may need to consider, such as the cost of daycare and transportation. If the parents decide to reduce income, however, they should appeal to the college financial aid administrator for a professional judgment review, since the prior tax year income will be higher than the income during the award year. The family should make the case that the reduced income more accurately reflects the family's current economic status compared to a prior year when the income was higher.

Repositioning Assets

Student vs. Parent Assets

Student assets are assessed at a greater rate than parent assets. Under the federal formula, dependent student assets are assessed at a flat 20% rate, so $10,000 in the student's name will reduce eligibility for need-based financial aid by $2,000. (In the formula used by the CSS/Financial Aid PROFILE form, student assets are assessed at a flat 25% rate.) In contrast, a portion of parent assets are sheltered by an asset protection allowance based on the age of the older parent. The asset protection allowance is between $30,000 and $60,000 for most parents of college-age children. The net worth of the family's principal place of residence, money in qualified retirement plans and the net worth of small businesses owned and controlled by the family are not reported as an asset. Any remaining reportable assets are assessed on a bracketed scale, with a top rate of 5.64%. In a worst-case scenario, $10,000 in the parent's name will reduce the student's eligibility for need-based financial aid by $564, an improvement of at least $1,436 in eligibility for need-based financial aid. So, it is always best to save for college in the parent's name, not the child's name.

If the child has some money in a custodial account, such as a Uniform Gift to Minors Act (UGMA) or Uniform Transfer to Minors Act (UTMA) account, there are several possible approaches to reducing the impact on eligibility for need-based financial aid.

- Roll the custodial account into a custodial 529 College Savings Plan account. Since July 1, 2009, custodial 529 plan accounts owned by a dependent student have been treated as a parent asset on the FAFSA. Contributions to a 529 plan must be made in cash, so this will require liquidating any investments in the child's name. Since that may result in capital gains, it is best to liquidate the child's investments two or more years prior to the child enrolling in college, as discussed above.

- Shift the child's money into the parent's name. Legally, the money is the property of the child, so the parents cannot simply move the money into their bank accounts. A minor child does not have the legal capacity to gift the money to his or her parents. It is best to consult with an accountant or financial planner about the proper way to shift the money. One approach is to spend the child's money for the child's benefit instead of using the parents' money. For example, if the child needs a SAT or ACT test prep class, a dorm refrigerator and microwave oven, a computer for school or a car to commute to college, pay for it with the child's money before filing the FAFSA. (Note, however, that college students may be able to qualify for a discount on computer equipment once they enroll.)

- Spend down child assets to pay for college before touching parent assets. This will prevent the child's assets from affecting eligibility for need-based financial aid in subsequent years. Parents sometimes want to spread out the child's money evenly over all four years, making up the difference with the parents' money, which yields a higher EFC than using up the child's money first.

Reportable vs. Non-Reportable Assets

Certain types of assets are not reportable as assets on the FAFSA. For example, money in a qualified retirement plan is not reported as an *asset* on the FAFSA. However, contributions to a retirement plan and distributions are reported as *income* on the FAFSA. So, while maximizing retirement plan contributions will shelter the money as an asset, it will not shelter it as income. Nevertheless, it is generally worthwhile to maximize retirement plan contributions in the years before the child enrolls in college to shelter as much money as possible. This is especially important because most people do not save enough money for retirement. At the very least, the parents should consider contributing enough to maximize the employer match, if any, since that's free money.

Small businesses owned and controlled by the family are not reported as assets on the FAFSA (but are reported as assets on the CSS/Financial Aid PROFILE form). One strategy might involve having the family business pay lower salaries to the family members. If the business is incorporated as a C corporation, the income retained by the business will not pass through to the federal income tax returns of the family members who own the business. The retained income will increase the net worth of the business, but the small family-owned business will not be reported as an asset on the FAFSA. In the interim, the family may be able to live off of savings.

Transferring title to investment real estate to a C corporation owned and controlled by the family might cause it to become a non-reportable asset on the FAFSA due to the small business exclusion.

Assets in the Name of a Younger Sibling

It is important to distinguish assets that are owned by a sibling from assets where the sibling is a beneficiary but not the owner of the assets.

Sibling-owned assets are not reported on a student's FAFSA. They are, however, reported on the CSS/Financial Aid PROFILE form. So, the benefits of putting assets in the name of a younger sibling are limited from a financial aid perspective. The assets will be assessed eventually, when the siblings enroll in college. However, if a sibling will not be enrolling in college for several years or if the sibling is a special-needs child, this strategy may be effective in sheltering the assets from need analysis.

Note that a 529 College Savings Plan, Prepaid Tuition Plan or Coverdell Education Savings Account owned by the parent must be reported as a parent asset on the FAFSA, even if the beneficiary is the student's sibling.

Avoid Grandparent-Owned 529 Plans

Although a 529 College Savings Plan owned by a grandparent is not reported as an asset on the FAFSA, any distributions from a grandparent-owned 529 plan will be reported as untaxed income to the beneficiary (the student) on the subsequent year's FAFSA. This can have a severe impact on eligibility for need-based aid. In contrast, a 529 plan owned by a dependent student or the student's custodial parent is reported as a parent asset on the FAFSA, which has a less severe impact on eligibility for need-based financial aid. Qualified distributions from a student- or parent-owned 529 plan are not reported as income on the FAFSA. Thus, it is usually better for the grandparents to contribute to a 529 plan owned by the student or parent than to open their own 529 plan.

If the grandparents have saved for their grandchildren in their own 529 plan, there are a few possible workarounds. One is to change the account owner of the 529 plan to be the parent. Another is to wait until the FAFSA is filed for the grandchild's senior year in college to take a distribution, when there will be no subsequent year's FAFSA to be affected by the distribution (assuming that the grandchild will not be enrolling in graduate or professional school).

The CSS/Financial Aid PROFILE form requires the applicant to report any 529 college savings plans for which the applicant is the beneficiary, even if the student and parents do not own the plan.

Accelerate Necessary Expenses

If the family needs a new car or the house needs a new roof or furnace, it may be better to spend the money on these necessary expenses before the children enroll in college than a few years later. Cars, computers, furniture, books, appliances, clothing and other personal property are

not reported as assets on the FAFSA. Home maintenance expenses are also not reported as assets on the FAFSA, since the net worth of the family's principal place of residence is not reported as an asset. If the parents are planning on buying these items anyway, accelerating their purchase may reduce reportable assets, thereby, decreasing the EFC. The family can also reduce reportable assets by making a charitable contribution.

Avoid Trust Funds

As discussed earlier, trust funds are generally ineffective at sheltering money from the need analysis formulas. The trust fund must still be reported as an asset even if there are restrictions on access to principal, unless the restrictions were established involuntarily by a court order.

Pay Down Debt

Similarly, paying down debt can help shelter money. Only debt that is secured by a reportable asset will reduce the net worth of the asset on the FAFSA. The FAFSA does not offset income or assets by unsecured consumer debt, such as credit card debt, and by debt secured by a non-reportable asset, such as a mortgage on the family's principal place of residence. Using extra money to pay down such debt will improve the student's eligibility for need-based financial aid. It may also save the family money, if the interest rate charged on the debt is higher than the interest rate earned on the savings. For example, if the parents carry a $5,000 balance on their credit cards, at 14 percent interest, and have $5,000 in a savings account earning one percent interest, paying off the credit card balance will save money by helping them avoid paying the higher interest rate on the credit card debt. The parents pay $700 in interest on the credit card but earn only $50 in interest on the savings account. It may also improve the student's eligibility for need-based financial aid by reducing the reportable assets by $5,000.

Note, however, that although the net worth of the family's principal place of residence is not reported as an asset on the FAFSA, it is reported as an asset on the CSS/Financial Aid PROFILE form. So, paying down mortgage debt may decrease the student's EFC under the federal need-analysis methodology, but perhaps not under the Institutional Methodology (IM).

Before pursuing such a strategy, however, the parents should save 3-6 months of salary in an emergency fund. The emergency fund might be used to cover living expenses if either or both parents lose their jobs or to cover other unforeseen expenses, such as furnace and car repairs. Some people recommend saving 6-12 months of salary in the emergency fund because the average time between jobs increased during the most recent economic downturn.

Avoid Home Equity Loans

The unspent proceeds of a home equity loan secured by the family home must be reported as an asset on the FAFSA. The proceeds are not reduced by the amount of the debt since the debt is secured by the family home, a non-reportable asset, and not by the cash proceeds.

This is in contrast with a home equity line of credit, where the cash does not exist until the borrower draws down on the line of credit.

There are, however, other reasons why the family might prefer one type of loan over the other, such as differences in interest rates, points and fees, differences in closing costs, differences in the repayment term, differences in the monthly payment and differences between fixed and variable interest rates.

Tweaking Demographic Information

Number in College

The number of children in college at the same time can have a big impact on the expected family contribution (EFC), since the parent contribution portion of the EFC is divided by the number of children in college. (The CSS/Financial Aid PROFILE form uses a different adjustment to the parental contribution when there are multiple children in college.) For example, twins, triplets and other multiples may qualify for more need-based financial aid than children who do not overlap in college. While it may be too late to implement such a family planning strategy, the impact on eligibility for need-based financial aid may influence the parents' thinking about whether to allow a child to skip a grade or take a gap year between high school and college.

Parents do not normally count in the number in college, ever since Congress changed the rules in 1992. However, if the parents are continuing their education at the same time as their children, they can appeal to the college financial aid administrator for a professional judgment review. The college financial aid administrator will generally want to see a list of the types and amounts of expenses, such as tuition, fees, books, supplies and equiment, with copies of paid bills and receipts. Some colleges will adjust the number in college or subtract the amount the family paid for the parent's education from the parents' income (minus employer-paid tuition assistance or other reimbursements of college costs), if they can verify that the parent is genuinely pursuing a college education.

It is also important to recognize that the number of children in college may change from one year to the next, affecting financial aid eligibility. For example, suppose a family has two children separated in age by one year. When the eldest child enrolls in college, the family will have just one child in college. The next year, they will have two children in college at the same time, potentially increasing the amount of financial aid for each of the children. When the youngest is a senior in college, however, the family will be back down to one child in college, increasing the family's EFC and, thereby, reducing the amount of financial aid.

Note that an increase in the number in college will not reduce the EFC when the parent contribution is less than about $1,000. While the parent contribution is divided by the number of children in college, the income protection allowance will decrease with each additional child in college. This yields an increase in available income that may offset the impact of splitting the parent contribution among multiple children when the parent contribution is already low.

Household Size

Household size also affects eligibility for need-based financial aid, but to a much lesser extent. However, families sometimes forget to count all members of their household. The most common errors include failing to count the student in the household size, failing to count an unborn child in household size, failing to count an adopted child and failing to count children who don't live in the home but who receive more than half their support from the parents. Do not, however, count foster children. Do not count other relatives or strangers who receive more than half their support from the parents but do not live in the home Also, while the family may regard a pet as a member of the family, pets cannot be counted in household size.

Divorce and Separation

When a student's parents are divorced or separated, only one parent is responsible for completing the FAFSA. The student may qualify for more need-based financial aid if this parent is the one with the lower income. (Note that the income of a stepparent must be included if the custodial parent has remarried.) To some extent, the parents can control which parent is responsible for completing the FAFSA by controlling where the student lives. This parent, called the custodial parent, is the parent with whom the student lived the most during the 12 months ending on the FAFSA submission date.

Dependency Status

Independent students may sometimes qualify for more aid than dependent students, since parent income and asset information are not reported on the FAFSA of an independent student. But, sometimes qualifying as an independent student will increase the EFC instead of decreasing it. The federal need-analysis methodology has three formulas, one for dependent students, one for independent students without dependents other than a spouse and one for independent students with dependents other than a spouse. Students who become independent through marriage may not necessarily qualify for more financial aid, especially if they substitute spouse income and assets for parent income and assets. Also, cash support from an independent student's parents must be reported as untaxed income to the student. (Cash support

includes money, gifts and loans, plus expenses paid by others on the student's behalf, such as food, clothing, housing, car payments or expenses, medical and dental care and college costs.) In any event, it is difficult for an otherwise dependent student to become independent. The main methods under the student's discretionary control are marriage, having a child or dependent other than a spouse, enlisting in the military, enrolling in graduate or professional school or waiting until age 24 to enroll in college. Dependency overrides, which are made at the discretion of the college financial aid administrator, are reserved for unusual circumstances that are unlikely to be under the student's discretionary control.

Based on data from the 2011-2012 National Postsecondary Student Aid Study (NPSAS), only 13.3% of undergraduate students under age 24 were independent in 2011-2012. (About seven eights (85.4%) of independent undergraduate students were independent because they were over age 24.) Of these, 54.5% were independent because they had dependents other than a spouse, 23.7% because they were married (15.0% because they were married and had no dependents other than a spouse), 5.2% because they were veterans and 2.5% because they were serving on active duty in the U.S. Armed Forces. Less than one percent were independent because of a dependency override.

Other Strategies

Federal Pell Grant Eligibility Limits

Students may receive Federal Pell Grants for the equivalent of 12 semesters (6 years of full-time enrollment). This restriction is based on the number of academic terms in which a Federal Pell Grant was received, not the amount of the Federal Pell Grant. If the student will be receiving a small Federal Pell Grant but expects to qualify for much larger grants in the future, it may be to the student's benefit to forgo receiving the Federal Pell Grant now to preserve future eligibility for the grant.

Maximizing Education Tax Credits

The American Opportunity Tax Credit provides a $2,500 tax credit based
on the first $4,000 in college tuition, required fees and course material
expenses. Since IRS rules prevent double-dipping, one cannot use a tax-
free scholarship or a tax-free distribution from a 529 College Savings Plan
to pay for expenses that justify the American Opportunity Tax Credit.
Instead, the parents will need to pay for these expenses with cash or
student loan money. This may affect the parent's strategy for spending
down student money first. The parents should consult with their tax
preparer, accountant or financial planner about how best to maximize
eligibility for the American Opportunity Tax Credit and other education
tax benefits.

Appeal for More Financial Aid

If the family has unusual financial circumstances, ask the college
financial aid administrator for a professional judgment review of those
circumstances. These can include changes in income or the net value of
assets from last year to the current year and anything that distinguishes
the family from the typical family. See the discussion of "Adjustments"
below for additional details about how to appeal for more financial aid.

CHANGES: CORRECTIONS, UPDATES AND ADJUSTMENTS

There are three types of changes that may be made to the information provided on the FAFSA: Corrections, Updates and Adjustments.

Corrections

After the FAFSA is submitted, the applicant may not change any information that was correct as of the date the FAFSA was submitted. The applicant may not modify any data elements to reflect changes that have occurred since the FAFSA was filed. For example, if the parent's brokerage account has lost value since the FAFSA filing date, the applicant may not change the parent assets reported on the FAFSA.

However, if the applicant made an error on the original FAFSA, the applicant may correct the error. The correction must be accurate as of the date the FAFSA was filed, not the date the information was changed.

For example, applicants may use the IRS Data Retrieval Tool to correct the income and tax data elements on the FAFSA.

Similarly, if an applicant transposed two digits in the parent asset figure, reporting $45,000 instead of $54,000, the applicant must correct the error.

An applicant may also add or remove colleges from the FAFSA or change his or her email address or mailing address. Changes in the PIN, email address and mailing address may not occur until the applicant's identity is confirmed with the Social Security Administration (SSA), which can take up to 3 days from the date the PIN is requested.

Be sure to sign and submit the corrected FAFSA after making any changes. The corrected FAFSA must be signed by the individuals whose information was changed. If the applicant, spouse and/or parents, as appropriate, do not sign the corrected FAFSA, an email reminder will be sent after seven days of inactivity.

Corrections may occur at any time before or during the award year.

If an applicant corrects an error on the FAFSA, other than through the IRS Data Retrieval Tool, the FAFSA is more likely to be selected for verification. If a FAFSA is selected for verification, the applicant and his or her parents, if applicable, will have to supply the college financial aid administrator with documentation of the figures reported on the FAFSA. Verification is intended to improve the accuracy of the FAFSA by reducing the number of errors on the form.

If a correction is submitted online, the correction will be processed in 3-5 days.

The applicant will receive a new Student Aid Report (SAR) after the corrections have been processed.

If the applicant wants to make additional corrections, he or she will need to wait until after he or she receives the SAR to make those corrections.

Updates

An update is a change to data elements on the FAFSA that were accurate as of the date the FAFSA was filed, but which have changed since the application date. Since the federal need analysis formula is based on a snapshot philosophy, most data elements on the FAFSA may not be updated. Some data elements may be updated, but only if the FAFSA is selected for verification.

In most cases, assets cannot be updated, as they must be accurate as of the date the FAFSA was filed. While FAFSA on the Web allows the applicant to change the asset information after the FAFSA is filed, this is intended to allow corrections of inaccurate information, not to permit correct information to be updated for changes that have occurred after the FAFSA was filed.

If an applicant's dependency status changes for any reason other than a change in the applicant's marital status, the applicant must update the dependency status on the form. Any data elements related to the change in dependency status must also be updated. For example, if both of a dependent student's parents die after the FAFSA is submitted, the student must update his or her dependency status to independent.

If a FAFSA is selected for verification of the household-size and/or number-in-college figures, the applicant must update those figures to be accurate as of the verification date, unless the update is due to a change in the applicant's marital status. These updates must occur regardless of whether the FAFSA was selected for verification by the U.S. Department of Education or by the college or university. These updates may not occur if the FAFSA is not selected for verification.

The financial aid administrator has the authority to require an update to the applicant's dependency status, household size and number in college due to a change in the applicant's marital status, if the financial aid administrator determines that the update is necessary to "address an inequity or to reflect more accurately the applicant's ability to pay." If the financial aid administrator allows an update due to a change in the applicant's marital status, all related data elements must also be updated, such as spousal income, taxes paid and assets. Financial aid administrators are permitted but not required to exercise this authority. Some financial aid administrators do not permit changes in the applicant's marital status. Others allow changes in the applicant's marital status, but may require applicants to appeal before a particular deadline date.

If a FAFSA is selected for verification, any changes to a dollar amount of $25 or more must be corrected. Any changes to a non-dollar data element must also be corrected. Material discrepancies of less than $25 do not need to be corrected as they usually do not result in a significant change in eligibility for need-based financial aid. (However, a change in income near the $50,000 threshold for the simplified needs test or the $24,000 threshold for auto-zero EFC may result in a significant change in aid eligibility.)

Adjustments and Overrides

The FAFSA is a one-size fits-all form. There is nowhere on the form where families can note unusual circumstances that affect their ability to pay for college. Instead, Congress allows college financial aid administrators to make adjustments to the data elements on the FAFSA and the college's cost of attendance, on a case-by-case basis, when supported by adequate documentation of *special circumstances*. Congress also granted college financial aid administrators the authority to perform dependency overrides from dependent student to independent student, when supported by documentation of *unusual circumstances*.

Adjustments are rare, with only about one percent of undergraduate students receiving an adjustment.

Special circumstances include anything that has changed from one year to the next and anything that distinguishes the family from the typical family.

Examples of special circumstances mentioned in the Higher Education Act of 1965[31] include:

- tuition expenses at an elementary or secondary school

- medical, dental, or nursing home expenses not covered by insurance

- unusually high child care or dependent care costs

- recent unemployment of a family member or an independent student

- a student or family member who is a dislocated worker

- the number of parents enrolled at least half-time in a degree, certificate, or other program leading to a recognized educational credential at an institution that is eligible for Title IV federal student aid

- a change in housing status that results in an individual being homeless

- other changes in a family's income, a family's assets, or a student's status

The Higher Education Act of 1965 also indicates that financial aid administrators may make adjustments

- to exclude from family income any proceeds of a sale of farm or business assets of a family if such sale results from a voluntary or involuntary foreclosure, forfeiture, or bankruptcy or involuntary liquidation

- to take into consideration the additional costs a student with a disability or a special needs student incurs as a result of the student's disability

The Higher Education Relief Opportunities for Students (HEROES) Act of 2003 (P.L. 108-76) allows college financial aid administrators to waive or modify any statutory or regulatory requirement relating to federal student aid in times of war, military operation or national emergency. Affected individuals include members of the military on active duty and their families, as well as individuals who live or work in an area that is declared a disaster area by a federal, state or local official in connection with a national emergency. The authority granted by the HEROES Act was subsequently made permanent.[32] The *Federal Register* mentions several waivers and modifications,[33] including:

- Substituting estimated award year income information (e.g., the first calendar year of the award year) for prior tax year information on the FAFSA

- Waive the requirement that adjustments be made on a case-by-case basis

Other common examples of adjustments granted by college financial aid administrators include:

- death, disability or serious illness of a wage earner

- incarceration or institutionalization of a wage earner

- mental or physical incapacitation of a wage earner

- a loss or reduction in parent or student income, including when a student quits a job to go to school full-time

- exclusion of one-time events from parent or student income (but not assets), such as the exclusion of an inheritance, unusual bonus, personal injury settlement or insurance settlement from income (but not from assets), because they are not reflective of the family's ability to pay during the award year

- natural disasters such as earthquakes, hurricanes, wildfires, tornados, floods and landslides

- loss or damage to the principal place of residence

- the end of child support when the child reaches the age of majority

- reductions in child support

- catch-up payments of child support owed from previous years

- the end of Social Security benefit payments

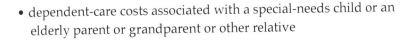

- dependent-care costs associated with a special-needs child or an elderly parent or grandparent or other relative

- exclusion of the conversion of a traditional IRA to a Roth IRA from income[34]

- exclusion of unusual capital gains, atypical one-time bonuses and worker's compensation buyouts

- exclusion of employer reimbursement of moving expenses that were included in income

- exclusion of hardship distributions from retirement plans, especially if used to pay for higher education expenses

- addressing volatile income by substituting an average of the last three years of income (e.g., taxi drivers, waitresses, commissioned sales staff and realtors all have income that may vary significantly from one year to the next)

- U.S. Armed Forces activation of a parent or student

Although not normally referred to as an adjustment, the Higher Education Act of 1965 allows college financial aid administrators to override a student's dependency status from dependent to independent when there are "unusual circumstances."[35] See the discussion of dependency overrides in Step 3 of Section 3.

To request an adjustment, the student or the student's parents (if the student is a dependent student) should call the school and ask about the school's process for a "professional judgment review." Some colleges call it a special circumstances review or a financial aid appeal. Some colleges will tell the family to write a letter requesting the review and to provide appropriate supporting documentation. Others will have a form that can be downloaded from the college's web site.

When writing a letter to request an adjustment, the letter should summarize the unusual circumstances affecting the family's ability to pay and discuss the financial impact of the unusual circumstances (including specific dollar amounts) on the family's ability to pay for college. The letter should also provide sufficient information for the financial aid administrator to identify the student, such as the student's name, the student's college ID number (if known), and the student's date of birth.

It is important to include copies of independent third-party documentation of the unusual circumstances, since the process is driven by documentation. Documentation can include copies of a layoff notice, proof of the recent receipt of unemployment benefits (within the last 90 days), copies of medical or dental bills and letters from doctors, clergy, social workers, child advocates, police, teachers, guidance counselors, college financial aid administrators and anyone else who is familiar with the student's situation. The documentation should ideally include information about the financial impact of the special circumstance in addition to discussing the nature of the special circumstance.

A professional judgment review should be requested from each of the colleges and universities to which the student is applying for admission and financial aid.

The appeal for more financial aid can occur at any time, even in the middle of the academic year. For example, if a parent loses his or her job in the middle of the school year, the family should ask for a professional judgment review at that time.

Most financial aid administrators will not make an adjustment in anticipation of a future change in the family's circumstances. Families should wait until the special circumstance has actually occurred to request a professional judgment review.

Each college's financial aid office will make its own decision about the request for an adjustment. Some colleges may make an adjustment while others may not. Decisions made by a financial aid administrator at one college are not binding on financial aid administrators at other colleges.

If the financial aid administrator feels that the unusual circumstances merit an adjustment, the amount of the adjustment will be related to the financial impact of the unusual circumstances on the family. For example, job loss will generally be implemented as a reduction in income, taking any severance pay or unemployment benefits into account. Adjustments for medical expenses may be reduced by the amount of medical expenses already considered by the federal need analysis methodology, which is 11 percent of the income protection allowance.

The changes in the data elements on the FAFSA will then result in a new expected family contribution (EFC). This, in turn, may result in a new financial aid package. (Note that even if the college allows an adjustment, the college may not be able to provide additional financial aid funds, but the financial aid administrator may be able to suggest other options.) So, the process is very formulaic.

Income Protection Allowance (IPA)

30%	Food
22%	Housing
9%	Transportation
16%	Clothing and Personal Care
11%	Medical Care
12%	Other Family Consumption

Financial aid administrators can also adjust the cost of attendance figures, not just the data elements on the FAFSA. For example, the financial aid administrator might increase the cost of attendance to include the cost of a computer, dependent care costs for a special-needs child or disability-related expenses. Financial aid administrators are more likely to adjust the cost of attendance when the student's EFC is zero, since current financial aid formulas do not allow the EFC to go below zero.

There are a few restrictions on the types of adjustments that may be granted by a financial aid administrator.

- Financial aid administrators cannot modify the financial aid formula, only the data elements that are part of the EFC calculation.

- Financial aid administrators cannot waive eligibility requirements. For example, if a student with a learning disability is enrolled on a half-time basis, the financial aid administrator may not award financial aid as though the student is enrolled full-time. On the other hand, they may waive the requirement that such a student be making satisfactory academic progress.[36]

- Financial aid administrators cannot modify the cost of attendance figure to include expenses that occur before enrollment (e.g., application and test fees) or after graduation (e.g., licensing fees).

Most financial aid administrators will generally not make adjustments for vacation expenses, tithing expenses, children's allowances, car payments, lawn care, gambling losses, mortgage payments, student loan payments or credit card payments. They will also not make adjustments to exclude assets that were transferred to the parent to enable a grandparent to qualify for Medicaid.

Adjustments for private school tuition apply only to tuition for a sibling's elementary and secondary school education. It does not include a sibling's college tuition, as that is addressed by the number in college. Some college financial aid administrators will, however, consider making an adjustment for extra costs associated with a special-needs child's college education, such as the cost of support services, transportation and other accommodations.

College financial aid administrators are more likely to make an adjustment when the unusual circumstance is due to factors beyond the family's control. They are less likely to consider an adjustment when the unusual circumstances are due to a discretionary choice made by the family. For example, even though private K-12 tuition for a sibling is mentioned in the Higher Education Act of 1965 as an example of a special circumstance, some financial aid administrators feel uncomfortable making adjustments for private tuition and fees. Other financial aid administrators will grant an adjustment, but cap it at the average cost to the government to educate a public school student (e.g., about $10,000 annually).

Most college financial aid administrators will perform a comprehensive review of the family's financial situation, not just the impact of the specific unusual circumstances. For example, if a dependent student's parent lost his job, but also won a multi-million dollar lottery, the financial aid administrator is unlikely to focus solely on the job loss.

Adjustments apply only to a single award year. Financial aid administrators must review the special circumstances once a year to ensure that they still apply before making an adjustment.

There is no appeal beyond the college financial aid administrator. Neither the college's president nor the U.S. Department of Education can override the financial aid administrator's decision. So, it pays to be polite. Honesty is always the best policy. If the financial aid administrator believes that the family is trying to game the system, the financial aid administrator can deny the appeal.

▶ Verification

In order to ensure that the information provided by students and parents is accurate, the U.S. Department of Education requires colleges and universities to verify the accuracy of financial and other demographic information provided on the FAFSA. Verification of FAFSA data helps colleges and universities accurately and equitably determine the types and amounts of federal, state and institutional funding students will receive.

The U.S. Department of Education uses a risk model to determine which FAFSAs will be selected for verification and the specific data elements that will be verified. The U.S. Department of Education publishes an annual notice [37] in the Federal Register that lists the data elements that may be selected for verification. These currently include:

- Adjusted Gross Income

- U.S. Income Tax Paid

- Untaxed Portions of IRA Distributions

- Untaxed Portions of Pensions

- IRA Deductions and Payments

- Tax Exempt Interest Income

- Education Credits

- Other Untaxed Income

- Income Earned from Work

- Number of Household Members

- Number in College

- SNAP benefits (formerly known as food stamps)

- Child Support Paid

- High School Completion Status

- Applicant Identity

About one-third of FAFSAs are selected for verification each year.[38]

An asterisk next to the expected family contribution (EFC) on the SAR is an indication that the student's FAFSA has been selected for verification.

Colleges may choose to select additional FAFSAs for verification and to verify additional data elements. Some colleges voluntarily verify 100 percent of the applications filed by their students.

Any data element that was provided by the IRS Data Retrieval Tool and not modified by the applicant will not be selected for verification.

Otherwise, the family will be required to complete IRS Form 4506-T, Request for Transcript of Tax Return, to have a tax transcript sent to the school. A tax transcript may also be requested online at www.irs.gov/Individuals/Order-a-Transcript or by calling 1-800-908-9946. Non-tax filers will be required to provide copies of W-2 or 1099 statements from each employer, if any income was earned from work, and to sign a statement confirming that they did not file a federal income tax return and were not required by the IRS to do so.

College financial aid administrators have the legal authority to request additional information and documentation when verifying a student's FAFSA. If the student and/or parents refuse to supply this information and documentation, the college may not disburse federal student aid funds to the student.

The U.S. Department of Education does not disclose the risk model used to select applications for verification. However, there are multiple scenarios that are likely to lead to verification:

- Taxes paid more than a specific percentage of adjusted gross income (AGI)

- Taxes paid are inconsistent with an estimate based on the adjusted gross income and the number of exemptions claimed on the federal income tax return

- FAFSA indicates that no tax return was filed, but income exceeds the IRS filing thresholds

- Marital status as reported on the FAFSA is inconsistent with marital status as reported on the federal income tax return, especially if the marital status on the FAFSA indicates that the parents have separated recently or the student got married recently

- FAFSA reports zero income or income insufficient to support the student (e.g., below the income protection allowance thresholds)

- FAFSA reports income that is inconsistent with the receipt of SNAP (formerly food stamps) or other means-tested federal benefit programs

- Household size on the FAFSA differs significantly from the number of exemptions claimed on the federal income tax return or is inconsistent with the dependency status questions

Technically, marital status on the FAFSA and marital status on the federal income tax return are not always the same. Marital status on the FAFSA is reported as of the date the FAFSA is filed. Marital status on the federal income tax returns is reported as of the last day of the tax year. If marital status changes between the end of the tax year and the FAFSA submission date, it is possible for the two to differ. However, changes in marital status in the few months between the last day of the tax year and the FAFSA application date are rare enough that discrepancies are often a sign of an error on either the FAFSA or the federal income tax return. (It is not uncommon for a taxpayer to incorrectly file federal income tax returns as married filing jointly with his or her boyfriend or girlfriend despite not being married.) When there is a discrepancy in the marital status on the two forms, the FAFSA is selected for verification to ensure that the change in marital status is genuine and not an error.

Conflicting Information

If there is a discrepancy between the information reported on the FAFSA and other information available to the college, including federal income tax returns, the financial aid administrator may not disburse federal student aid funds until the conflicting information is resolved. The financial aid administrator is also precluded from making an adjustment as part of a professional judgment review until the conflicting information is resolved. If the FAFSA was selected for verification, the financial aid administrator may not disburse federal student aid funds until verification is complete.

Conflicting information may be resolved by correcting the FAFSA, correcting the document that conflicts with the FAFSA or by demonstrating that there is no conflict. For example, suppose that the FAFSA indicates that the student is single, but the student filed a federal income tax return as married. The conflicting information could be resolved by documenting that the student got divorced after the end of the tax year and before filing the FAFSA. Otherwise, the student might have to file an amended federal income tax return (IRS Form 1040X) or correct the information on the FAFSA to resolve the discrepancy.

Common examples of conflicting information include:

- The student, spouse (if the student is married) or parents (if the student is a dependent student) indicate on the FAFSA that they are not required to file a federal income tax return, but the earned income reported on the FAFSA exceeds the IRS filing thresholds.

- The federal income tax return lists dividend and interest income, but no assets were reported on the FAFSA, or the reported amount of assets is inconsistent with the amount of dividend and interest income or capital gains.

- The dependent student's permanent address does not match the address listed on the custodial parent's federal income tax return.

- The student's parents are divorced and the custodial parent is unmarried, yet no child support is reported on the FAFSA or no alimony is reported on the federal income tax return.

- Both of a student's parents filed federal income tax returns as head of household.

If the student, the student's parents (if the student is a dependent student) or the student's spouse (if the student is married) refuse to complete verification, refuse to provide documentation requested by the college's financial aid administrator or refuse to help resolve conflicting information, the college cannot disburse federal student aid funds.[39]

Common Errors to Avoid

Students should double-check the FAFSA before submitting it to make sure they haven't made any errors. The following are some of the most common errors on the FAFSA.

General Errors

- The most common error occurs when the student, the custodial parent (if the student is a dependent student) or the student's spouse (if the student is married) fails to sign the FAFSA.

- Another common error is failing to file the FAFSA because the family feels it won't qualify for aid, the family feels the form is too complicated or time-consuming or the applicant feels that he or she can work his or her way through school.

- Leaving a data field blank on the paper FAFSA, instead of entering a zero ("0").

- Using commas or decimal points in dollar figures on the FAFSA. Amounts should be rounded to the nearest dollar. Dollar amounts on the FAFSA are written without cents.

- Digit or letter transpositions. It is surprising how often applicants will swap two adjacent digits in their Social Security Number or telephone number or have a typo in their name.

- Including an extra zero, especially in dollar amounts, or duplicating a digit. Writing $500,000 instead of $50,000 or $511,000 instead of $51,000 can have a big impact on the expected family contribution (EFC).

- Don't miss deadlines. Applicants should not wait until after they have filed their federal income tax returns or have been admitted to a college or university to file the FAFSA. Some colleges and

states have very early deadlines for filing the FAFSA. Some award aid on a first-come, first-served basis until the money runs out.

- Don't file the wrong year's FAFSA. Depending on the time of year, there may be FAFSAs available for two different years: the current award year and the next award year. A student who is applying for financial aid for the fall should file the FAFSA for that award year, not the previous year, as soon after January 1 as possible.

- If you are confused, ask for help. Call 1-800-4-FED-AID (1-800-433-3243) with questions about the FAFSA.

Data Match Errors

- Using the wrong Social Security Number will cause a data match error on the FAFSA. This can include substituting the Social Security Number of a sibling for the student or swapping the student and parent Social Security Numbers. Another variation is using a Taxpayer Identification Number (TIN) for someone who does not have a Social Security Number. If a parent does not have a Social Security Number because the parent is not a U.S. citizen or permanent resident, use 000-00-0000 as his or her Social Security Number. Do not make up a Social Security Number or use a stolen Social Security Number.

- Failing to use the student and parents' correct legal names. The name on the FAFSA must match the name on the Social Security card. Do not use a nickname or informal name. If the Social Security card uses a maiden name, use that name on the FAFSA. Then, contact the Social Security Administration (www.ssa.gov) to get the legal name updated in its records.

- Failing to write the first and last names in the correct fields. Students sometimes get confused because the FAFSA asks for the last name first.

- Errors in the date of birth. Surprisingly, some parents misremember the year in which they were born. Don't substitute the current year for the year of birth. Write the date of birth in the order month, day, year (MM/DD/YYYY), not day, month, year (DD/MM/YYYY).

- Citizenship match failures. The student's Social Security Number is used to check the student's citizenship status. Sometimes, students who have become U.S. citizens or permanent residents after entering the United States have not contacted the Social Security Administration to have the citizenship status associated with their Social Security Number updated.

- Wrong address. The address listed on the FAFSA should be the student's permanent home address, not the campus address or a temporary summer address. Ideally, this address should be the same as the one used on federal income tax returns.

Errors Involving Taxes

- The FAFSA asks for the federal income tax figure from a specific line of the federal income tax return. Do not report the total tax figure, which includes other taxes. Do not add self-employment tax to the total. Do not use the total payments figure from the federal income tax return. Do not use the income tax refund amount. Do not report the amount of taxes withheld on the W-2 form.

- Some applicants accidentally report their adjusted gross income (AGI) in the federal income tax field, since the two data elements are adjacent. The FAFSA will be rejected if the federal income tax is equal to the AGI.

- Applicants who have not yet filed their federal income tax returns may be tempted to report the total income tax withholding figures from the last pay stub of the year. This figure may vary significantly

from the actual federal income tax figure; similarly, for total estimated tax payments. Using the federal income tax figure from the previous year's federal income tax return will usually be more accurate if the adjusted gross income from the prior year is close.

- Incorrectly claiming head of household status. If the student or parents filed income tax returns with the wrong filing status, they will have to file amended federal income tax returns (IRS Form 1040X) before the college can disburse the student aid funds. This can cause delays in the awarding of financial aid.

- Specifying the wrong type of income tax return. Taxpayers who filed an IRS Form 1040 but were eligible to file an IRS Form 1040A or 1040EZ should check the box for IRS Form 1040A or 1040EZ. (Note that a taxpayer who itemizes deductions is not considered eligible to file an IRS Form 1040A or 1040EZ, even if that was the only reason why the taxpayer filed an IRS Form 1040. A taxpayer who files IRS Form 1040 only to claim the earned income tax credit, the American Opportunity Tax Credit or the Lifetime Learning Tax Credit may check the box for IRS Form 1040A or 1040EZ.)

Errors Involving Income

- Incorrect income earned from work. Some applicants will report the same figure for adjusted gross income (AGI) and income earned from work. These figures are unlikely to be the same, since adjusted gross income adds unearned income to the total and subtracts various exclusions from income.

- The earned income tax credit is not the same as income earned from work, despite the similarity of the names.

- The FAFSA asks for the taxable portion of certain forms of need-based student aid so that they can be excluded from income. Note that income reported on the FAFSA is based on the tax year (usually the calendar year), not the academic year.

- Supplemental Security Income (SSI) is not the same as Social Security Disability Insurance (SSDI). Do not confuse them, even though the acronyms are similar.

- When reporting contributions to qualified retirement plans, show only the employee's contributions. Do not show the employer's contributions.

Errors Involving Assets

- Report the net value of assets as of the date the FAFSA is filed, not necessarily the end of the most recent calendar year.

- Qualified retirement plans and the net worth of the family home are not reported as assets on the FAFSA. Do not include these assets in the response to the question about the net worth of investments.

- College savings plans of siblings (and the student) are reported as assets of the parent if the custodial parent is the account owner. This includes 529 College Savings Plans, Prepaid Tuition Plans and Coverdell Education Savings Accounts.

- If a noncustodial parent, grandparent, aunt, uncle or other relative is the owner of a college savings plan, do not report it as an asset on the FAFSA (but do report it on the CSS/Financial Aid PROFILE form). Distributions from such a college savings plan, however, are reported as untaxed income to the beneficiary (the student).

- Assets are reported on the FAFSA as an asset of the account owner, not the beneficiary. The only exception is for custodial college savings plan accounts, which are reported as a parent asset on the FAFSA if the student is a dependent student.

- Rental properties are normally reported as investment assets, not business assets, unless they are part of a formally recognized business.

- Applicants who qualify for the simplified needs test should ask their colleges if assets should be reported. Some states and colleges use asset information when determining eligibility for state and institutional aid funds.

Errors Involving Dependency Status

- Some students have difficulty with date arithmetic and get confused by the question that asks whether they were born before January 1. If the birth year is less than the year specified in this question, answer "Yes."

- Students who served on active duty for *training purposes* are not considered veterans for federal student aid purposes. Members of the National Guard or Reserves who have not been called to *national* active duty are not considered veterans. Likewise, ROTC students are not considered veterans.

- If a student serves on active duty, even for one day, and was discharged with a character of service other than "Dishonorable," the student is considered a veteran for federal student aid purposes. Note that a student who has a character of service of "Under Other than Honorable Conditions" is considered a veteran for federal student aid purposes.

- If a student has a child, but the child receives more than half his or her support from the student's parents, the student is not considered to have a legal dependent other than a spouse.

Errors Involving Marital Status

- Marital status must be reported as of the date the FAFSA is filed. Do not anticipate a future change in marital status. Do not report marital status as of the end of the tax year or calendar year if it has changed since then.

- A student who is separated but not divorced is still considered married with regard to the dependency status question, "As of today, are you married?"

- If a student's parents are divorced or separated, only one parent is responsible for completing the FAFSA. This parent, referred to as the *custodial parent*, is the parent with whom the student lived the most during the 12 months ending on the date the FAFSA is submitted, or, if the student lived equally with both parents, the parent who provided more financial support. This is not necessarily the same as the parent who has legal custody or the parent who claimed the student as an exemption on his or her federal income tax return. For example, multiple support agreements do not affect which parent is responsible for completing the FAFSA.

- If a student's parents are divorced, the question about parent marital status refers to the marital status of the custodial parent who is completing the FAFSA. If the custodial parent has remarried, the parent marital status is "Married," not "Divorced or Separated."

- If a student's parents are divorced and the custodial parent has remarried, the stepparent must be counted in household size and his or her income and assets must be reported on the FAFSA, regardless of whether there is a prenuptial agreement.

- Students or parents (if the student is a dependent student) who are in a same-sex marriage should identify themselves as married on the FAFSA if they were legally married in a state or foreign country that permits same-sex marriage.

- If one of the student's parents has died, report only the income and assets of the surviving parent. Do not include the income and assets of the deceased parent.

Errors Involving Household Size

- Failure to report unborn children. If a child will be born before the end of the award year and will receive more than half support from the student or parents (if the student is a dependent student), the unborn child should be counted in household size. Do not, however, report an unborn child based on an *anticipated* pregnancy. There must be medical documentation of a *current* pregnancy to count an unborn child in household size.

- If a stepparent has children from a previous marriage, those children should be counted in household size if the stepparent provides more than half of their support and will continue to do so throughout the award year, even if the children do not live with the stepparent.

- If the student's parents are unmarried but living together, any children who receive more than half support from the parents (or who would be deemed to be a dependent of the parents if they were filing a FAFSA) should be counted in household size.

- Sometimes applicants fail to count themselves in household size or number in college. Always count the student even if he or she is going away to college.

Errors Involving Prior Education

- Be careful when answering the question about having received a Bachelor's degree prior to July 1, as answering "Yes" can cause the student to become ineligible for the Federal Pell Grant and other forms of federal student aid.

- A high school diploma is not a college degree or certificate.

- The question about the parents' educational attainment is used to identify students who are the first in their family to go to college. If neither parent has earned a Bachelor's degree or a more advanced degree, this question may make the student eligible for more financial aid. Answer "High school," not "College or beyond," if the parent has some college but does not have a Bachelor's degree. This question is designed to match all possible definitions of a "first-generation college student." Some states define a first-generation college student as a college student whose parents do not have a Bachelor's degree, while others define a first-generation college student as a college student whose parents do not have an Associate's degree or a Certificate.

- A professional degree is not a degree from a vocational program at a technical school. It is an advanced degree in law (J.D. or L.L.B.), medicine (M.D. or D.O.), veterinary medicine (D.V.M.) or similar advanced fields.

Errors that May Affect Aid Eligibility

- Always answer "Yes" to the question about interest in Federal Work-Study. Answering "No" does not increase the amount of grant aid the student will receive. Students can always turn down Federal Work-Study or scholarship funds later.

- Failing to register with Selective Service. Male students aged 18 to 25 who fail to register with Selective Service may be ineligible for federal student aid, as well as some state and institutional student aid.

Errors Involving Unusual Circumstances

- If filing a paper FAFSA, do not write notes in the margins or include anything with the FAFSA. The margin notes will be ignored and may cause scanning errors. When mailing, do not include anything with the paper FAFSA, as it will not be read. If there are unusual family financial circumstances, bring them to the attention of the college financial aid administrator by contacting the financial aid office in writing and asking for a professional judgment review.

Errors Involving a Failure to Finish

- Failing to list a college on the FAFSA. If a college is not listed on the student's FAFSA, it will not receive the data from the FAFSA and might not consider the student for federal, state or institutional financial aid funds.

- Failing to submit the FAFSA after adding a new school or using the IRS Data Retrieval Tool to update the FAFSA.

- Failing to sign the FAFSA. If completing FAFSA on the Web (FOTW), use a PIN to sign the form. Applicants can also print the signature page, sign it and mail it to the address listed on the signature page. If the student is a dependent student, both the student and a custodial parent must sign the FAFSA.

RECEIVING FINANCIAL AID FUNDS

Generally, within two weeks after a student arrives on campus, financial aid funds will be disbursed to the student. (In some cases, financial aid funds may be credited to the student's account up to 10 days before the first day of classes.) Federal student aid funds – including federal student loans, the Federal Parent PLUS Loan, Federal Work-Study, the Federal Pell Grant and other federal grants – are disbursed through the school.

The school first applies the federal student aid funds to institutional charges for tuition and fees, as well as room and board (if the student is living in campus-owned housing). Any remaining money must be refunded to the student to pay for textbooks, supplies, computer equipment and software, and miscellaneous/personal expenses. Typically, this will happen within 14 days. However, student loan funds are subject to a few special rules:

- Students must receive "entrance counseling" before receiving federal student loan funds.

- There is a 30-day delay before student loan funds may be disbursed for first-year, first-time borrowers.

- Student loan funds must be disbursed in at least two installments, once per pay period (e.g., per academic term).

The last two rules may be waived at colleges that have a low student loan default rate.

CONCLUSION

Filing the FAFSA for the first time can be intimidating, but this book has, hopefully, made the process simpler and easier to understand and complete.

Please consider submitting a question for publication in the *Ask the Edvisor* column at www.edvisors.com/ask/ask-the-edvisor/. Questions may be submitted about any topic related to planning and paying for college, including filing the FAFSA. Due to the high volume of questions, the authors are not able to respond to every question. Questions that are of a more widespread potential interest are more likely to be selected for publication. Questions may be edited for content, clarity and style. The person asking the question may be identified in the published question and answer using his or her first name and/or initials.

APPENDICES

Differences between Federal and Institutional Financial Aid Formulas

The financial aid formula used by the FAFSA to calculate the student's expected family contribution (EFC) is known as the Federal Need Analysis Methodology or Federal Methodology (FM).

Some colleges use a different formula for awarding their own financial aid funds. This formula is known as an Institutional Methodology (IM). The CSS/Financial Aid PROFILE form is used by about 250 mostly-private colleges and a similar number of scholarship competitions to calculate an EFC under the institutional methodology. The PROFILE form gathers answers to many more questions than the FAFSA. Each college and university that uses the PROFILE form may modify the formula.

The most common differences between FM and IM are summarized in this table:

Financial Aid Formula Components	FM	IM (CSS/Financial Aid PROFILE)
Net Worth of Family Home	Ignored	Capped, usually at 2-3 times income
Simplified Needs Test	Yes	No
Net Worth of Small Family Businesses	Ignored	Counted
Minimum Student Contribution or Summer Work Expectation	No	Yes
Paper Losses (Depreciation, capital losses, business/farm losses, NOL carry-forwards)	Counted	Ignored
Non-Custodial Parent Income/Assets	Ignored	Counted
Number of Children in College	Equal split of parent contribution	Smaller reduction in parent contribution
Assets Owned by a Sibling	Ignored	Counted, if sibling is under age 19 and not yet in college
Allowance for College Savings	None	Subtracted from assets
Allowance for Emergency Reserve	None	Subtracted from assets
Start of Application Season	January 1	October 1
Adjustment for Regional Cost of Living Differences	No	Yes
Assessment of Student Assets	20%	25%

FM and IM have different adjustments to the parental contribution when more than one child is enrolled in college at the same time.[40] The parent contribution is multiplied by the percentages listed in this table.

Number in College	FM	IM (CSS/Financial Aid PROFILE)
1	100%	100%
2	50%	60%
3	33%	45%
4	25%	35%

Glossary

Acronyms

A.A.	Associate of Arts Degree
A.S.	Associate of Science Degree
AAI	Adjusted Available Income
AFDC	Aid to Families with Dependent Children (replaced by TANF)
AGI	Adjusted Gross Income
AI	Available Income
AMT	Alternative Minimum Tax
APA	Asset Protection Allowance
ARN	Alien Registration Number (A-Number)
ARRA	American Recovery and Reinvestment Act of 2009
ATB	Ability-to-Benefit
ATI	Allowances against Total Income
ATM	Automatic Teller Machine
AY	Academic Year or Award Year
B.A.	Bachelor of Arts Degree
B.S.	Bachelor of Science Degree

CAI	Contribution from Available Income
CCRAA	College Cost Reduction and Access Act of 2007
CFR	Code of Federal Regulations
COA	Cost of Attendance
COD	Common Origination and Disbursement System
COTW	Corrections on the Web
CPA	Certified Public Accountant
CPS	Central Processing System
CSS	College Scholarship Service
CWS	College Work-Study
DACA	Deferred Action for Childhood Arrivals
DCL	Dear Colleague Letter
DHS	U.S. Department of Homeland Security
DL	Direct Loans
DNW	Discretionary Net Worth
DOB	Date of Birth
DOMA	Defense of Marriage Act
DRN	Data Release Number, a 4-digit number
DRT	IRS Data Retrieval Tool

ECASLA	Ensuring Continued Access to Student Loans Act of 2008
ED	U.S. Department of Education
EEA	Employment Expense Allowance
EFC	Expected Family Contribution
EFT	Electronic Funds Transfer
EIC	Earned Income Credit
EIN	Employer Identification Number
FAA	Financial Aid Administrator
FAFSA	Free Application for Federal Student Aid
FAO	Financial Aid Office
FAT	Financial Aid Transcript (replaced by NSLDS)
FC	Foreign Country
FERPA	Family Educational Rights and Privacy Act of 1974
FFELP	Federal Family Education Loan Program
FHFA	Federal Housing Finance Agency
FICA	Federal Insurance Contributions Act
FM	Federal Methodology
FOTW	FAFSA on the Web

FSA	Federal Student Aid
FSAIC	Federal Student Aid Information Center
FSEOG	Federal Supplemental Educational Opportunity Grant
FTC	Federal Trade Commission
FWS	Federal Work-Study
GED	General Educational Development Certificate
GPA	Grade Point Average
HCERA	Health Care and Education Reconciliation Act of 2010
HEA	Higher Education Act of 1965
HELOC	Home Equity Line of Credit
HEOA	Higher Education Opportunity Act of 2008
HERA	Higher Education Reconciliation Act of 2005
HEROES Act	Higher Education Relief Opportunities for Students (HEROES) Act of 2013
HSA	Health Savings Account
I-551	Permanent Resident Card (Green Card)
I-551C	Conditional Permanent Resident Card
I-94	Arrival-Departure Record
IM	Institutional Methodology

INS	Immigration and Naturalization Service (now known as USCIS)
IPA	Income Protection Allowance
IPEDS	Integrated Postsecondary Education Data System
IRA	Individual Retirement Account
IRS	Internal Revenue Service
ISIR	Institutional Student Information Record
LEU	Lifetime Eligibility Used
LIBOR	London Interbank Offered Rate
LIHEAP	Low Income Home Energy Assistance Program
MPN	Master Promissory Note
NDSL	National Defense Student Loan (now known as Federal Perkins Loan)
NSLDS	National Student Loan Data System
OIG	Office of the Inspector General
OMB	Office of Management and Budget
OPE	Office of Postsecondary Education
P.L.	Public Law
PC	Parent Contribution
PCA	Parent Contribution from Assets

PCI	Parent Contribution from Income
PII	Personally Identifiable Information
PIN	Personal Identification Number
PJ	Professional Judgment
PY	Prior Year
PPY	Prior Prior Year
R2T4	Return of Title IV Funds
RA	Research Assistantship
ROTC	Reserve Officers' Training Corps
SAFRA	Student Aid and Fiscal Responsibility Act
SAP	Satisfactory Academic Progress
SAR	Student Aid Report
SC	Student Contribution
SCA	Student Contribution from Assets
SEOG	See FSEOG
SEP	Simplified Employee Pension Plan
SFA	Student Financial Assistance
SIC	Dependent Student's Income Contribution
SID	Student Identifier (for COD)

SIMPLE	Savings Incentive Match PLan for Employees
SNAP	Supplemental Nutrition Assistance Program (previously known as Food Stamps)
SNT	Simplified Needs Test
SSA	Social Security Administration
SSDI	Social Security Disability Insurance
SSI	Supplemental Security Income
SSN	Social Security Number
SSS	Selective Service System
STX	State and Other Tax Allowance
TA	Teaching Assistantship
TANF	Temporary Assistance for Needy Families
TDD	Telephone Device for the Deaf
TEACH	Teacher Education Assistance for College and Higher Education Grant
TI	Total Income
TIN	Taxpayer Identification Number
TIV	Title IV of the Higher Education Act of 1965
TSP	Thrift Savings Plan
TTY	Teletype

UGMA	Uniform Gift to Minors Act
USC	United States Code
USCIS	U.S. Citizenship and Immigration Services
USED	U.S. Department of Education
UTMA	Uniform Transfer to Minors Act
VA	U.S. Department of Veterans Affairs
WIA	Workforce Investment Act
WIC	Special Supplemental Nutrition Program for Women, Infants and Children
YTD	Year-To-Date

Definitions

Visit www.edvisors.com/glossary/ for a more comprehensive glossary of college admissions and financial aid terminology.

1040
IRS Form 1040 is a federal income tax return for individual taxpayers.

1040A
IRS Form 1040A is a shorter version of IRS Form 1040 for individual taxpayers who satisfy certain restrictions, such as limitations on the types of income received by the taxpayer and limitations on the types of adjustments to income. Taxpayers who file IRS Form 1040A also cannot itemize their deductions.

1040EZ
IRS Form 1040EZ is a simplified version of IRS Form 1040A for taxpayers who have no dependents.

1098-E
IRS Form 1098-E is used to report student loan interest paid by a borrower.

1098-T
IRS Form 1098-T is used to report tuition and fees paid by a taxpayer. These payments may entitle the taxpayer to claim education tax credits or certain exclusions from income.

1099
IRS Form 1099 is used to report income other than wages, salaries and tips. It may be used to report income paid to an independent contractor, interest and dividend income, and implied income from the cancellation of debt.

1099-C
IRS Form 1099-C is used to report implied income from the cancellation of debt.

1099-DIV
IRS Form 1099-DIV is used to report dividends and other distributions from investments.

1099-INT
IRS Form 1099-INT is used to report interest income from a bank deposit.

1099-MISC
IRS Form 1099-MISC is used to report miscellaneous income.

1099-Q
IRS Form 1099-Q is used to report payments from qualified education programs.

1099-R
IRS Form 1099-R is used to report distributions from pensions, annuities and retirement plans (including 401(k), 403(b) and IRA plans).

2555 or 2555EZ
IRS Form 2555 is used to report foreign earned income that is exempt from U.S. income tax.

401(k)
A 401(k) plan is a type of retirement savings plan. Contributions are made by employees using before-tax exclusions from income. Some employers may match employee contributions. Earnings grow tax-free.

403(b)
A 403(b) plan is a type of retirement savings plan typically offered by non-profit employers and public education organizations.

4506-T
IRS Form 4506-T is used to order a tax transcript from the IRS. Taxpayers may also order a tax transcript online or call 1-800-908-9946.

4868

IRS Form 4868 is used by taxpayers to apply for an automatic extension of the time to file a U.S. federal income tax return.

529 College Savings Plan (529 Plan)

529 College Savings Plans are state-sponsored investment plans that help families save money for college. The plans have tax benefits so savings can grow faster. The money in the accounts can be used only for qualified education expenses. 529 College Savings Plans, Prepaid Tuition Plans and Coverdell Education Savings Accounts are collectively called Qualified Tuition Programs (QTP).

Above-the-Line

The term "above-the-line" refers to the calculation of the taxpayer's adjusted gross income (AGI). If an exclusion from income occurs above-the-line, it affects the calculation of AGI. Itemized deductions occur below-the-line and do not affect the calculation of AGI.

Academic Transcript

A transcript is a record of a student's academic performance.

Academic Year

An academic year is the school year of an educational institution. Most colleges and universities have an academic year that runs from August or September to May or June.

Access

The term "access" refers to the concept of enabling low-income or other at-risk students to pursue a postsecondary education. Financial aid improves access by eliminating demonstrated financial need as a barrier to a college education.

Accrues

Interest is said to accrue or accumulate on a loan.

Adjusted Available Income

Adjusted Available Income (AAI) is the income that remains after allowances for taxes, employment expenses and basic living expenses have been subtracted.

Adjusted Gross Income

Adjusted Gross Income (AGI) is total income, including both earned and unearned income, after subtracting certain exclusions from income, but before subtracting deductions and exemptions.

Adjustment

An adjustment is a change to data elements on the FAFSA that are used to calculate the expected family contribution (EFC). An adjustment can also be a change to the cost of attendance (COA). Adjustments occur at the discretion of the college financial aid administrator after a case-by-case review of documented special circumstances.

Admit-Deny

A student is said to be in an admit-deny situation when the college offers admission to the student but fails to award enough financial aid for the student to be able to afford to enroll.

Alien

An alien is a citizen of a foreign country, not the country in which the individual resides.

Alimony

Alimony is court-ordered support paid by a husband or wife to his or her former spouse after divorce or separation.

Appeal

A financial aid appeal is a request for more financial aid, usually because of special circumstances that affect the family's ability to pay.

Arrears
Child support obligations that are owed and unpaid are said to be in arrears. Past-due child support obligations do not affect eligibility for federal student aid.

Asset
An asset is something of monetary value. It may include tangible and intangible property.

Asset Protection Allowance
The Asset Protection Allowance (APA) shelters a portion of assets from being assessed by the need analysis formula. The APA is based on the age of the older parent if the applicant is a dependent student and the older of the student and the student's spouse if the applicant is an independent student.

Assistantship
An assistantship is a form of financial aid where the student performs services in exchange for a full or partial tuition waiver and a living stipend. The most common types of assistantships are research assistantships and teaching assistantships.

Associate's Degree
An Associate's Degree is awarded by two-year colleges, such as community colleges.

Auto-Zero EFC
Low-income students who are eligible to file an IRS Form 1040A or 1040EZ or who receive certain means-tested federal benefits will have their EFC automatically set to zero.

Award Letter
A financial aid award letter (also called a financial aid notification) is a paper or electronic document from a college that describes the types and amounts of financial aid offered to the student. The award letter also explains the terms of the financial aid, what the student is expected to do to keep the award and a deadline for accepting the award.

Award Year
An award year is a 12-month period that runs from July 1 to June 30.

Bachelor's Degree
A Bachelor's degree is awarded by four-year colleges and universities.

Base Year
The base year is the prior tax year (calendar year). Applicants report income earned during the base year on the FAFSA. For example, if a student is applying for financial aid for the 2015-2016 award year, the base year is 2014.

Bracket
A bracket refers to figures associated with a range of income. For example, a tax bracket is an income range that is taxed at a particular rate.

Budget
See Student Budget.

Bursar
The bursar is the college official or office responsible for handling billing and payments for tuition, fees, housing and other related expenses.

Cafeteria Plan
A cafeteria plan is a type of employee benefit under section 125 of the Internal Revenue Code. These benefits are excluded from income, except when the plan discriminates in favor of highly compensated employees or more than a quarter of the benefits accrue to key employees. Contributions to a cafeteria plan and payments from a cafeteria plan are not reported as untaxed income on the FAFSA.

Calendar Year
A calendar year is a 12-month period that runs from January 1 to December 31.

Campus-Based Aid
Campus-based aid includes the Federal Perkins Loan, Federal Work-Study and Federal Supplemental Educational Opportunity Grant programs.

Capital Gains
Capital gains refers to the profit from the sale of an investment or other asset.

Capital Losses
Capital losses refers to the loss from the sale of an investment or other asset.

Case-by-Case
A case-by-case professional judgment review considers each student's situation separately from all others. College financial aid administrators may not have broad policies or practices that treat all students the same, regardless of the details of the student's circumstances.

Cash Support
Cash support includes money, gifts and loans, plus expenses paid by others on the student's behalf, such as food, clothing, housing, car payments or expenses, medical and dental care and college costs.

Certificate
A certificate is an education credential awarded for completion of a one-year program.

Clergy
A member of the clergy is an official of a religious group or order. Examples of clergy include priests, bishops, pastors, ministers, rabbis, imam and ayatollah.

Cohabit
A couple is said to cohabit when they live together.

Combat Pay
Combat pay is a form of hazard pay for soldiers who are deployed to a combat zone or engaged in active combat.

Common Application
The Common Application is a standard college admissions application form accepted by more than 400 colleges that are members of the Common Application Association.

Common-Law Marriage
A common-law marriage is a marriage established by mutual agreement and cohabitation, as opposed to a ceremony performed by an authorized person in front of witnesses.

Community Property
Community property is property owned jointly by husband and wife.

Completion
Completion of a degree or certificate program occurs when the student receives the degree or certificate, typically during a graduation ceremony.

Conflicting Information
Conflicting information is any discrepancy or inconsistency in the information provided to a college, including information from the FAFSA and federal income tax returns.

Cost of Attendance
A college's cost of attendance includes the cost of tuition, fees, room, board, books, supplies, equipment, transportation, loan fees, dependent-care costs, disability-related costs and miscellaneous/personal expenses.

Coverdell Education Savings Account
A Coverdell Education Savings Account is a tax-advantaged account for saving for qualified K-12 and higher education expenses. Contributions are limited to $2,000 per year through age 18.

CSS/Financial Aid PROFILE
The CSS/Financial Aid PROFILE is a financial aid application created by the College Scholarship Service of the College Board. The PROFILE is used by more than 400 colleges, universities and private scholarship programs to award their financial aid funds.

Custodial Account
A custodial account is established to hold assets on behalf a minor.

Custodial Parent
The custodial parent is the parent with whom the student lived the most during the 12 months ending on the FAFSA application date. If the student lived equally with both parents, the custodial parent is the parent who provided more support to the student during the 12 months ending on the FAFSA application date or the most recent calendar year during which either parent provided the student with some support.

Data Release Number
The Data Release Number (DRN) is a four-digit number listed in the upper right hand corner of an online Student Aid Report (SAR) and in the lower left hand corner of a paper SAR. Providing the DRN to a college will allow the college to access the FAFSA data. The DRN can also be provided to the Federal Student Aid Information Center (FSAIC) to allow them to correct errors in the FAFSA or add schools to the FAFSA.

DD-214
A DD-214 is a document issued by the U.S. Department of Defense to members of the U.S. Armed Forces upon the servicemember's retirement or discharge from active-duty service.

Dear Colleague Letter
A Dear Colleague Letter (DCL) is a form of subregulatory guidance provided by the U.S. Department of Education to colleges, lenders, states and guarantee agencies.

Defense of Infancy
The defense of infancy argues that an underage child lacks the capacity to enter into legal contracts.

Demonstrated Financial Need
Demonstrated financial need is the difference between the cost of attendance (COA) and the expected family contribution (EFC).

Dependency Override
A dependency override changes a student's status from dependent to independent. College financial aid administrators may perform a dependency override on a case-by-case basis when justified by documented unusual circumstances.

Dependency Status
A student's dependency status is either dependent or independent.

Dependent Student
A dependent student is a student who does not qualify as an independent student. Dependent students must report parental income and asset information on the FAFSA.

Depreciation
Depreciation occurs when the value of an asset is reduced over the useful life of the asset.

Disbursement
Disbursement is the payment of student aid funds. After student aid funds are applied to institutional charges such as tuition, fees, room and board, any remaining funds are refunded to the student to pay for other college costs, such as books, supplies, transportation and miscellaneous/personal expenses.

Dislocated Worker
A dislocated worker is an employee who has been laid off or received a layoff notice from his or her job because of a permanent closure of, or substantial layoff at, a plant, facility, or enterprise, or who is employed at

a facility where the employer has announced that the facility will close within 180 days, or who is receiving unemployment benefits due to being laid off and is unlikely to return to a previous occupation, or who is self-employed but is unemployed due to economic conditions or a natural disaster, or who is a displaced homemaker. Note that employees who voluntarily quit their jobs are not considered to be dislocated workers.

Displaced Homemaker

A displaced homemaker is someone who previously provided unpaid servicers to the family, such as a stay-at-home parent, who was supported by income from another family member but is no longer supported by that income, who is unemployed or underemployed, and who is having trouble finding or upgrading employment.

Distribution

A distribution is the withdrawal of money from an account. Distributions from retirement plan accounts may include taxable and untaxed income.

Dividend

A dividend is a periodic payment from a company to its shareholders.

Divorce

Permanent legal ending of a marriage.

Documentation

Documentation is a record of information or evidence.

Early Action

Early action (EA) is a non-binding form of early admission to college. Students admitted in an early action program usually have until May 1 to decide if they will attend a specific college or university.

Early Decision

Early decision (ED) is a binding form of early admission to college. The applicant has committed to enrolling in the college if he or she is admitted as part of the early decision application pool.

Earned Income

Earned income is money paid for services, typically in the form of salary, wages and tips.

Eligible Noncitizen

An eligible non-citizen is an individual who is a U.S. national (native of American Samoa, Swain's Island or the U.S. Minor Outlying Islands), a U.S. permanent resident who has an I-151, I-551 or I-551C Permanent Resident Card, or someone with an Arrival-Departure Record (I-94) from the U.S. Citizenship and Immigration Services (USCIS) showing one of the following designations: Refugee; Asylum Granted; Cuban-Haitian Entrant, Status Pending; Conditional Entrant (valid only if issued before April 1, 1980); Victims of human trafficking with a T Visa (T-2, T-3 or T-4, etc.); or Parolee who has been paroled into the United States for at least one year for other than a temporary purpose with the intent to become a U.S. citizen or permanent resident.

Elite College

An elite college is a very selective or prestigious college.

Emancipation

Emancipation occurs when a minor child is released from the control of his or her parents, usually upon reaching the age of majority. An emancipated minor is a child who is released from the control of his or her parents prior to reaching the age of majority.

Enrollment Status

A student's enrollment status indicates whether the student is enrolled full-time or part-time. A student must be enrolled on at least a half-time basis to qualify for federal student loans. The Federal Pell Grant is available on a prorated basis to students who are enrolled less than half-time. Campus-based aid and the TEACH Grant do not require half-time enrollment.

Equity

Equity is the dollar amount of a person's financial interest in a property, generally equal to the market value of the property minus any debt secured by the property.

Exclusion

An exclusion from income is a deduction that occurs before calculation of the AGI.

Expected Family Contribution

The expected family contribution (EFC) is a measure of the family's financial strength. It is calculated based on the FAFSA and is a minimum measure of the family's share of college costs. It is used to determine the student's eligibility for student financial aid in the calculation of financial need. Despite the name, it is not the amount of money the family will pay for college. Most families will pay more than the EFC because some colleges do not provide enough student financial aid to cover the student's full demonstrated financial need. Even among the colleges that cover full demonstrated financial need, the financial aid package may include loans and/or student employment.

Family Educational Rights and Privacy Act of 1974 (FERPA)

The Family Educational Rights and Privacy Act of 1974 (FERPA) protects the privacy of educational records, including financial aid application forms. FERPA does not allow colleges and universities to reveal parent financial information to the student.

Federal Family Education Loan Program (FFELP)

The Federal Family Education Loan (FFEL) program made federal education loans that were funded and serviced by banks and other financial institutions and guaranteed against default by the U.S. Department of Education. The FFEL program ended on June 30, 2010. All new federal education loans made on or after July 1, 2010 have been made through the Direct Loan program.

Federal Methodology (FM)

The Federal Methodology is a standardized formula, defined by federal law, for determining a student's (and family's) ability to pay for postsecondary education expenses. The formula is also used to determine an Expected Family Contribution (EFC) for the Federal Pell Grant, campus-based and Federal Direct Loan programs.

Federal Pell Grant
The Federal Pell Grant program is the largest federal grant program to help students pay for college.

Federal Perkins Loan
The Federal Perkins Loan is a fixed-rate loan for students with exceptional financial need.

Federal PLUS Loan
The Federal PLUS Loan is borrowed by parents of undergraduate students (Parent PLUS) or by graduate and professional school students (Grad PLUS).

Federal Processor
The federal processor receives FAFSA applications, performs edit checks to ensure consistency of the data, performs database matches to verify eligibility, calculates a student's expected family contribution (EFC), produces the student's SAR and ISIR and processes corrections, updates and adjustments to the FAFSA data.

Federal Stafford Loan
The Federal Stafford Loan is the largest federal student loan program. Federal Stafford loans may be subsidized, where the government pays the interest that accrues during periods of authorized deferment, or unsubsidized, where the borrower is responsible for the interest that accrues.

Federal Student Aid Information Center
The Federal Student Aid Information Center (FSAIC) is a toll-free hotline, 1-800-4-FED-AID (1-800-433-3243), which answers questions about federal student aid and the FAFSA. It is sponsored by the U.S. Department of Education.

Federal Student Aid PIN

The Federal Student Aid PIN or FSA PIN is four-digit number used to electronically sign an online FAFSA. It can also be used to sign the Master Promissory Note (MPN) and access other U.S. Department of Education web sites. The FSA PIN is obtained at www.pin.ed.gov.

Federal Work-Study

Federal Work-Study is a need-based part-time student employment program.

Financial Aid

Financial aid is money given, earned or loaned to help pay for college. Financial aid can come from federal and state governments, colleges, businesses, and private and social organizations.

Financial Aid Administrator

A financial aid administrator (FAA) is a college employee who administers student financial assistance programs and counsels families about how to pay for college costs.

Financial Aid Notification

See Award Letter.

Financial Aid Package

A financial aid package is a collection of multiple types of financial aid from multiple sources to help the student pay for college. The financial aid package is described in the financial aid award letter.

Financial Need

See Demonstrated Financial Need.

Fiscal Year

The federal government's fiscal year is a 12-month period that runs from October 1 to September 30.

Free Application for Federal Student Aid
The Free Application for Federal Student Aid (FAFSA) is a financial aid application form used to apply for student financial aid from the federal and state governments and most colleges and universities.

Front-Loading
Front-loading is a strategy employed by some colleges to award more grants and scholarships to a student in his or her first year of attendance. In subsequent years, the college will reduce the amount of grants and scholarships and offer more self-help aid, such as student employment and student loans.

Full-Time
A full-time student carries a full-time academic workload, which typically involves at least 12 credit hours per academic term or 24 clock hours per week.

Gapping
Gapping occurs when a student is left with unmet demonstrated financial need.

Gift Aid
Gift aid is money that does not need to be repaid, such as grants, scholarships and tuition waivers.

Grade Point Average
A student's Grade Point Average (GPA) is a measure of the student's academic performance, typically reported on a 4.0 scale. An 'A' grade corresponds to a 4.0, a 'B' grade to a 3.0, a 'C' grade to a 2.0. Students must maintain at least a 2.0 GPA to retain eligibility for federal student aid.

Graduate Student
A graduate student pursues a higher-level education, such as a Master's degree or a doctoral degree, after receiving a Bachelor's degree.

Graduation Rate

The graduation rate is the percentage of students receiving a degree or certificate within 150% of the normal timeframe for attaining a degree or certificate (e.g., 6 years for a 4-year program).

Grant

A grant is a type of gift aid, money that does not need to be repaid. Grants are usually awarded based on demonstrated financial need.

Guardian

See Legal Guardian.

Half-Time

A half-time student carries half of the academic workload of a full-time student. Recipients of federal education loans must be enrolled on at least a half-time basis. Recipients of the Federal Pell Grant, TEACH grant and campus-based aid may be enrolled less than half-time.

Homeless

A homeless student does not have a fixed, regular and adequate place of nighttime residence.

Homemaker

A homemaker is a stay-at-home parent who manages the household and cares for the children.

Household

A household is a group of people who live together as a family. The federal need analysis methodology includes children in a parent's household if they receive more than half their support from a parent even if they don't live with the parent.

Incarceration

An incarcerated student is serving a prison sentence. Incarcerated students may have more limited eligibility for federal student aid. Incarcerated students are not eligible for federal student loans. Students imprisoned in a federal or state penal institution are not eligible for the Federal Pell Grant, while students imprisoned in other penal institutions are eligible for the Federal Pell Grant. These eligibility restrictions are removed when the student is released from prison. However, students who have a conviction for the sale or possession of illegal drugs while enrolled in college or who are subject to an involuntary civil commitment for a sexual offense may have limitations on their eligibility for federal student aid.

Income
See Earned Income and Unearned Income.

Independent Student
An independent student is not required to provide parental income and asset information on the FAFSA. Independent student status is defined by the Higher Education Act of 1965 as including students who are age 24 as of December 31 of the award year, married, have dependents other than a spouse, have children, are on active duty in the U.S. Armed Forces, are veterans of the U.S. Armed Forces, are graduate or professional school students, are an orphan or ward of the court, are in a legal guardianship, are in foster care, are an emancipated minor or are an unaccompanied youth who is homeless or who is self-supporting and at risk of becoming homeless. College financial aid administrators may also use a dependency override to change a student's dependency status from dependent to independent in unusual circumstances.

Individual Retirement Account
An individual retirement account (IRA) plan is a type of retirement savings plan. Contributions to a traditional IRA are made by employees using before-tax exclusions from income. Contributions to a Roth IRA are made by employees using after-tax income.

Institution of Higher Education
Colleges and universities are postsecondary institutions of higher education.

Institutional Methodology (IM)
An institutional methodology is a financial aid formula used by a college or university to award its own financial aid funds.

Institutional Student Information Record
The Institutional Student Information Record (ISIR) is a set of database records containing the information in a student's Student Aid Report (SAR), including financial and demographic information and the student's expected family contribution (EFC).

Internal Revenue Service
The Internal Revenue Service (IRS) is the federal agency responsible for processing federal income tax returns and for collecting and refunding tax payments from taxpayers.

Ivy League
A group of eight elite colleges: Brown University, Columbia University, Cornell University, Dartmouth College, Harvard University, Princeton University, the University of Pennsylvania, and Yale University.

Legal Dependent
A legal dependent is a child who receives more than half of his or her support from the student, including biological, adopted and unborn children. The children do not have to live with the student. Legal dependents also include other people, other than a spouse, who currently live with *and* receive more than half their support from the student and will continue to do so through the end of the award year.

Legal Guardian
A legal guardian has been granted legal custody of another person, such as a child whose parents are incapacitated or deceased.

Loan
A loan is money borrowed from the government, a bank or another source. Loans must be repaid, usually with interest, over a specific period of time.

Major
A major is an academic field of study.

Matriculate
A student matriculates when he or she enrolls in college.

Means-Tested
A means-tested benefit is provided to an individual based on the individual's income and assets.

Merit
Academic, artistic or athletic talent.

Merit-Based Aid
Merit-based aid is financial aid awarded to students based on their personal achievements. Most scholarships are considered merit aid, as they are generally awarded for success in school, the arts, athletics or another area.

Methodology
A methodology is a financial aid formula.

Naturalization
Naturalization is the process through which a foreign citizen or national is granted citizenship.

Need
See Demonstrated Financial Need.

Need Analysis
Need analysis is a process that evaluates household income, asset and demographic information to determine the family's financial strength and ability to pay for school.

Need-Aware Admissions
A college has a need-aware or need-sensitive admissions policy if it considers the student's ability to pay alongside other criteria while deciding whether to admit the student.

Need-Based Aid

Need-based aid is awarded to students based on demonstrated financial need, to help them pay for the cost of college. Need-based aid usually comes in the form of grants, student employment opportunities and student loans. Most need-based aid comes from the federal and state governments, as well as from colleges and universities.

Need-Blind Admissions

A college has a need-blind admissions policy if the college admits students without regard to their demonstrated financial need. Some colleges that are need-blind become need-sensitive when admitting international students, transfer students and wait-listed students. Not all need-blind colleges meet the full demonstrated financial need of admitted students. This leads to an "admit-deny" situation in which the student is admitted but the college does not provide the student with the financial aid the student needs to be able to afford to attend the college.

Need-Sensitive Admissions

See Need-Aware Admissions.

Net Cost

Net cost is the difference between the college's full cost of attendance and the full financial aid package, including loans. The actual cost to the family will be higher, since loans have to be repaid.

Net Price

Net price is the difference between the college's full cost of attendance and only the gift aid a student receives. This is the true amount of money a student will pay to attend a college. It is the equivalent of a discounted sticker price.

Net Price Calculator

A net price calculator is an online tool that provides a personalized estimate of what it will cost to attend a specific college. Most colleges are required by law to provide a net price calculator on their web sites.

Net Value
See Net Worth.

Net Worth
The net worth of an asset is the difference between the market value of the asset and any debts secured by the asset.

Noncustodial Parent
If a student's parents are divorced, one parent is the custodial parent and the other parent is the noncustodial parent.

Orphan
An orphan is a child both of whose biological parents are dead.

Outside Scholarship
See Scholarship.

Override
See Dependency Override.

Package
See Financial Aid Package

Parent
A parent is the student's adoptive or biological mother or father. If the student's parents are divorced and the custodial parent has remarried, the federal definition of parent includes the stepparent.

Parent Contribution
The parent contribution is an estimate of the parents' ability to contribute to the cost of attendance of a dependent student. The expected family contribution is the sum of the student contribution and parent contribution.

Pell Grant
See Federal Pell Grant

Per Capita
Per capita is the portion attributable to each person.

Perkins Loan
See Federal Perkins Loan

Postsecondary
Education beyond high school.

Postsecondary Institution
A postsecondary institution is a college or university, or vocational or trade school.

Prenuptial Agreement
A prenuptial agreement is a contract executed by a couple prior to getting married. The prenuptial agreement typically specifies spousal support and the division of property upon divorce. A prenuptial agreement may also be called an antenuptial agreement or premarital agreement.

Prepaid Tuition Plan
A prepaid tuition plan is a form of college savings plan where an investor purchases shares that represent a fixed percentage of future college tuition.

Preponderance of Evidence
A preponderance of evidence occurs when there is more evidence in favor of a conclusion than against it.

Principal Balance
The principal balance of a loan is the outstanding balance upon which interest is charged.

Principal Place of Residence
A family's principal place of residence is the family's home.

Prior Prior Year

Prior Prior Year (PPY) refers to the year before the prior tax year. Under current law, financial aid eligibility is based on income during the prior year, but not the prior prior year. Policymakers have considered proposals to shift the base year from the prior year to the prior prior year, since this would allow students to apply for financial aid before applying for college admissions, instead of afterward.

Prior Tax Year

The prior tax year is the tax year (usually a calendar year) that ends before the award year. For example, applications for financial aid for the 2015-2016 award year will be based on income and tax data from the 2014 tax year.

Prior Year

See Prior Tax Year and Base Year.

Priority Date or Deadline

The priority date or deadline is the date by which an application — whether it's for college admission, student housing or financial aid — must be received to be given the strongest consideration.

Private Scholarship

See Scholarship.

Procrastinate

To procrastinate is to delay or postpone taking action.

Professional Judgment

Professional judgment is the process by which a college financial aid administrator reviews, on a case-by-case basis, special circumstances affecting a student's ability to pay for college. During a professional judgment review, the financial aid administrator may decide to make an adjustment to the cost of attendance or to the data elements on the FAFSA that are used to calculate the student's expected family contribution (EFC).

Professional School
A professional school is a college or university offering advanced degrees in law, medicine, dentistry, veterinary medicine, pharmacy, optometry, podiatry, osteopathic medicine, chiropractic medicine or business.

PROFILE
See CSS/Financial Aid PROFILE

Refund
A refund is money disbursed to the student from a student's account at the college after the student aid funds are applied to institutional charges, such as tuition and fees, leaving a credit balance in the account.

Reserve Officers' Training Corps (ROTC)
ROTC is a program offered by the military and available at some colleges. ROTC offers scholarships to students who agree to serve in the military after they graduate. The program combines a military education with college study leading to a bachelor's degree.

Residency Requirement
A residency requirement is the amount of time a student has to live in a state before he or she is eligible for in-state tuition prices and state aid at public colleges and universities.

Retention Rate
The retention rate is the percentage of first-time, first-year undergraduate students who return to the college the next year.

Roth IRA
A Roth IRA is a type of retirement account in which after-tax money is invested and earnings grow on a tax-deferred basis. Qualified distributions are tax-free after the account owner reaches age 59 1/2.

Satisfactory Academic Progress

Satisfactory academic progress includes quantitative and qualitative measures of a student's progress to a degree or certificate. Students must generally maintain at least a 2.0 GPA on a 4.0 scale and be passing enough classes to graduate within 150 percent of the normal timeframe for the degree.

Scholarship

A scholarship is a form of gift aid, money that does not need to be repaid. Scholarships are usually awarded by private organizations (e.g., foundations, corporations, associations, individual philanthropists and nonprofit organizations) based on some form of merit, such as academic, artistic or athletic talent, or activities, such as community service. Also called Private Scholarships or Outside Scholarships.

Secondary School

A secondary school is a high school.

Selective Service

Male U.S. citizens and immigrants age 18-25 are required to register with the Selective Service System. Male students who fail to register may be ineligible for federal, state and, frequently, institutional student financial aid for college.

Self-Help Aid

Self-help aid includes financial aid in the form of student employment and student loans.

Separation

A legal separation is a court-ordered agreement in which husband and wife remain married but live apart. An informal separation is not court-ordered. An informal separation is sometimes called a trial separation.

Sibling

A sibling is a brother or sister.

Signature Page
The signature page is a document that can be printed and signed instead of using a PIN to sign the FAFSA. Signing the FAFSA with a PIN is faster.

Simplified Needs Test
The Simplified Needs Test (SNT) ignores assets from the calculation of a student's EFC for low- and moderate-income students who are eligible to file an IRS Form 1040A or 1040EZ or who are eligible for certain means-tested federal benefit programs.

SNAP
The Supplemental Nutrition Assistance Program (SNAP), previously known as food stamps, provides nutrition assistance to low-income individuals and families.

Special Circumstances
Special circumstances include significant changes in a family's financial circumstances from one year to the next or circumstances that differentiate the family from the typical family. Examples include job loss, salary reduction, death of a wage-earner, high unreimbursed medical and dental expenses, high dependent care costs and private elementary and secondary school tuition for a sibling.

Stafford Loan
See Federal Stafford Loan

Statement of Educational Purpose
The statement of educational purpose is an agreement by the student to use federal student financial aid funds for educational expenses only.

Stepparent
A stepparent is a stepfather or stepmother. A stepparent is a parent by marriage, not birth. For example, a stepfather is the husband of a child's natural mother after the death or divorce of the child's natural father.

Sticker Price
A college's sticker price is the college's cost of attendance, including tuition, fees, room and board, before any student financial aid is subtracted from the total.

Student Aid
Student aid is financial aid funding provided to a student to enable him or her to pay for a college education. See also Financial Aid.

Student Aid Report
The Student Aid Report (SAR) summarizes the information submitted on the FAFSA and includes the student's EFC.

Student Contribution
The student contribution is an estimate of the student's ability to contribute to his or her cost of attendance. The expected family contribution is the sum of the student contribution and parent contribution.

Student Employment
Student employment is a program that allows students to take a part-time job, on- or off-campus, as part of their financial aid package.

Student Financial Aid
See Student Aid.

Subsidized
A student loan is subsidized if the federal government pays the interest on the loan during periods of authorized deferment, such as during the in-school deferment and the economic hardship deferment.

TANF
Temporary Assistance for Needy Families (TANF) is a federal assistance program that provides cash assistance to low-income families with dependent children. It replaced the Aid to Families with Dependent Children (AFDC) program.

Tax Credit
Tax credits directly reduce the amount of taxes paid by a tax filer.

Tax Deduction
Tax deductions reduce the amount of an individual's income that is taxed.

Tax Exemption
A tax exemption excludes a form of income from taxes. For example, interest earned on municipal bonds is exempt from federal income tax.

Tax Transcript
A tax transcript is a record of the income, tax and demographic information received by the IRS from a taxpayer on his or her federal income tax return.

TEACH Grant
The TEACH Grant is a forgivable loan that requires the recipient to work as a teacher in a national need area for a specified number of years after graduation. Although identified as a grant, it converts retroactively to an unsubsidized Federal Stafford Loan if the recipient fails to fulfill the service requirement.

Testamentary
Established by a deceased person's last will and testament.

Title IV
Title IV refers to federal student aid programs authorized under Title IV of the Higher Education Act of 1965.

Total Income
Total income is the sum of taxable income (the adjusted gross income) and untaxed income.

Transcript
See Academic Transcript.

Transfer Rate
The transfer rate is the percentage of the first-time, first-year undergraduate students who transfer to another college within 150 percent of the normal timeframe for attaining a degree or certificate.

Transfer Student
A transfer student is a student who enrolls in a college after having attended another college.

Tuition
Tuition is the cost charged to students for academic instruction at a college or university.

Undergraduate Student
An undergraduate student is pursuing a Certificate, Associate's degree or Bachelor's degree. Undergraduate education typically does not exceed four years of academic study beyond a high school diploma.

Unearned Income
Unearned income is money received not for work, such as interest, dividends and capital gains.

Unmet Need
Unmet need is the difference between the student's demonstrated financial need and the student's financial aid package. Unmet need may also be referred to as a "gap."

Unsubsidized
The interest on an unsubsidized loan is the responsibility of the borrower. The government does not pay the interest on an unsubsidized loan.

Untaxed Income
Untaxed income includes all income received that is not reported to the Internal Revenue Service (IRS) or is reported to the IRS but excluded from taxation. Such income includes, but is not limited to, untaxed retirement

plan distributions, untaxed capital gains, interest on tax-free bonds and dividend exclusion, as well as military and other subsistence and living allowances.

Upperclassmen
Upperclassmen include sophomores, juniors and seniors.

Verification
If a student's FAFSA is selected for verification, the college financial aid administrator will compare the information submitted on the FAFSA with independent documentation of the information, such as IRS tax transcripts and W-2 and 1099 forms.

Veteran
A veteran for federal student aid purposes is a student who has served on active duty for at least one day in the U.S. Armed Forces (Army, Navy, Air Force, Marines, Coast Guard), who is a member of the National Guard or Reserves who was called to active national duty for purposes other than training, who enrolled at one of the service academies or who enrolled at a U.S. military academy preparatory school. The student must also have been discharged with a character of service other than "Dishonorable" (or will be by the end of the award year).

Veterans Administration
The Veterans Administration (VA), also known as the U.S. Department of Veterans Affairs, is a cabinet-level federal agency that serves the needs of military veterans, including veterans education benefits and health care.

W-2
IRS Form W-2, the Wage and Tax Statement, is used to report income from wages, salaries and tips, and the amount of taxes withheld. Employers must mail the W-2 statements to employees by January 31.

Ward of the Court
A child is a ward of the court if the court has taken legal custody of the child.

References

[1] See the Bureau of Labor Statistics http://www.bls.gov/emp/ep_chart_001.htm; Mark Kantrowitz, The Financial Value of a Higher Education, Journal of Student Financial Aid, 37(1), 2007 http://www.nasfaa.org/research/Journal/subs/The_Financial_Value_of_a_Higher_Education.aspx; The College Payoff http://cew.georgetown.edu/collegepayoff/; What's It Worth http://cew.georgetown.edu/whatsitworth/; Projections of Jobs and Education Requirements through 2018 http://cew.georgetown.edu/jobs2018/; Table 6 on page 106 of http://www.bls.gov/opub/mlr/2012/01/art5full.pdf; Education Pays http://trends.collegeboard.org/education-pays; and Cancer Mortality in the United States by Education Level and Race http://jnci.oxfordjournals.org/cgi/doi/10.1093/jnci/djm127.

[2] Total Student Aid and Nonfederal Loans in 2013 Dollars, in Excel, http://trends.collegeboard.org/

[3] Based on Summary of Enhancements to the 2014-2015 Free Application for Federal Student Aid (FAFSA) Oct 2013 http://www.regulations.gov/#!documentDetail;D=ED-2013-ICCD-0061-0002. "Consistent with the Supreme Court decision on the Defense of Marriage Act (DOMA), same-sex couples must report their marital status as married if they were legally married in a state or other jurisdiction (foreign country) that permits same-sex marriage." United States v. Windsor (2013, Docket No. 12-307) http://www.supremecourt.gov/opinions/12pdf/12-307_6j37.pdf.

[4] 34 CFR 668.37(a)(2)

[5] Alabama, Colorado, Idaho, Louisiana, New Hampshire, South Dakota, and Tennessee

[6] Alaska, Arizona, Arkansas, California, Delaware, Florida, Georgia, Idaho, Illinois, Kentucky, Maine, Massachusetts, Mississippi, Missouri, Montana, New Hampshire, New Jersey, North Carolina, North Dakota, Ohio, Oklahoma, Texas, Utah, Virginia, West Virginia, and Wisconsin.

[7] See http://www.sss.gov/qa.htm#quest35.

[8] 20 USC 1091(d), as amended by the Consolidated Appropriations Act of 2012 (P.L. 112-74).

9 2014-15 Federal Student Aid Handbook, Volume 1, Chapter 6, page 1-67.

10 20 USC 1091(r) http://www.law.cornell.edu/uscode/text/20/1091#r.

11 See, for example, http://www.insidehighered.com/news/2013/10/28/colleges-use-fafsa-information-reject-students-and-potentially-lower-financial-aid.

12 See page 64 of Completing the FAFSA 2013-14, http://studentaid.ed.gov/sites/default/files/2013-14-completing-fafsa.pdf.

13 DCL GEN-11-15 http://ifap.ed.gov/dpcletters/GEN1115.html

14 See 34 CFR 668.55 and 75 FR 66832.

15 http://thomas.loc.gov/cgi-bin/bdquery/z?d100:H.R.558:.

16 42 USC 11434A(2)(A).

17 42 USC 11302(a)(2).

18 20 USC 1087oo(f)(1)

19 20 USC 1087oo(f)(3).

20 20 USC 1087oo(f).

21 A joint 2004 study by the IRS and US Department of Education discovered that about 4 percent of Pell Grant recipients had different information on FAFSAs and federal income tax returns, even after verification

22 A homemaker is considered to be underemployed if he or she is working part-time but seeking full-time work or whose current employment is below the level of his or her education or job skills

23 See margin note on page AVG-19 of the 2013-14 Application and Verification Guide. Reported on line 25 of IRS Form 1040.

[24] 20 USC 1087vv(e) and 20 USC 1087vv(b)(2).

[25] Others include the Free and Reduced Price School Lunch, Commodity Supplemental Food Program (CSFP), Special Milk Program for children, WIA educational benefits.

[26] The foreign income exclusion was removed from the definition of untaxed income by the College Cost Reduction and Access Act of 2007.

[27] The Higher Education Opportunity Act of 2008 changed the treatment of veterans education benefits to no longer treat them as a resource (reducing aid dollar for dollar) or otherwise have them affect eligibility for need-based financial aid.

[28] 20 USC 1087vv(g).

[29] Note that cash, checking and savings accounts, money market accounts and CDs all function the same on the FAFSA.

[30] The current treatment of 529 plans was implemented by the College Cost Reduction and Access Act of 2007, effective starting with the 2009-10 award year.

[31] 20 USC 1087tt(a)

[32] P.L. 110-93

[33] Federal Register 68(239):69312-69318, December 12, 2003, extended by Federal Register 70(202):61037, October 20, 2005.

[34] DCL GEN-99-10

[35] 20 USC 1087vv(d)(1)(l)

[36] 34 CFR 668.16(e), 34 CFR 668.32(f) and 34 CFR 668.34.

[37] See http://www.ifap.ed.gov/dpcletters/GEN1316.html for a link

[38] Data provided by the U.S. Department of Education indicates that from 1/1/2013 to

11/1/2013, 5,722,505 of the 18,827,577 FAFSAs submitted to date were selected for verification. That's 30.4%. An additional 1.07% were selected because of an unusual enrollment history. The number selected for verification each year tends to vary by a few percent.

[39] HEA Section 479A(a). 34 CFR 668.51(b), 34 CFR 668.54(a)(3), 34 CFR 668.54(a)(5), 34 CFR 668.60(a), 34 CFR 668.60(b)(1), 34 CFR 668.60(c)(2) and 34 CFR 668.60(d). Also 34 CFR 668.16(f), 34 CFR 668.16(g)(1) and HEA section 490(a) and (d).

[40] http://www.collegeboard.com/prod_downloads/highered/res/pj_tips/siblings.pdf

Quick Reference Guide

Web Sites

www.fafsa.ed.gov
Online version of the Free Application for Federal Student Aid (FAFSA)

www.pin.ed.gov
Web site for obtaining a PIN to sign the FAFSA electronically

www.collegegoalsundayusa.org
College Goal Sunday, a source of free help completing the FAFSA

www.sss.gov
Selective Service System

www.ssa.gov
Social Security Administration

www.edvisors.com
Edvisors.com is a web site about planning and paying for college

http://profileonline.collegeboard.org
The CSS/Financial Aid PROFILE form.

www.federalreserve.gov/releases/h10/current/
Federal Reserve Board web page that lists official currency exchange rates

www.irs.gov
Internal Revenue Service (IRS)

www.irs.gov/Individuals/Order-a-Transcript
IRS web site for ordering a tax transcript

www.nces.ed.gov/collegenavigator
College Navigator

www.gibill.va.gov
Montgomery GI Bill

www.americorps.gov
AmeriCorps

http://collegecost.ed.gov
College Affordability and Transparency Center

Telephone Numbers

For questions about the FAFSA or federal student aid:
1-800-4-FED-AID (1-800-433-3243) or 1-319-337-5665.
TDD/TTY 1-800-730-8913.

To apply for a Social Security Number or correct errors:
1-800-772-1213. TDD/TTY 1-800-325-0778

To order a federal income tax transcript from the IRS:
1-800-908-9946

To check a student's Selective Service registration:
1-888-655-1825 or 1-847-688-6888.

To report fraud involving federal student aid funds:
1-800-MIS-USED (1-800-647-8733)

Important Dates

October 1	First day for filing the PROFILE
January 1	First day for filing the FAFSA
February (1st Sunday)	IRS Data Retrieval Tool becomes available
April 15	Federal income tax returns due
May 1	National Candidates Reply Date